Shakespeare
Made Easy

Muriel J. Morris

J. Weston Walch, Publisher
Portland, Maine

1   2   3   4   5   6   7   8   9   10

ISBN 0-8251-2412-3

Copyright © 1990
J. Weston Walch, Publisher
P.O. Box 658 • Portland, Maine 04104-0658

Printed in the United States of America

Contents

To the Teacher

"Ewwh!"

"Ugh!"

"Why do we hafta?"

"Yuk!"

We've heard that before: the sound of Shakespeare-resistance. My students seem to feel honor-bound to make derisive noises when I introduce a Shakespeare unit (even if they've never studied Shakespeare before), perhaps because they've heard Shakespeare is hard or boring or "dumb." Admittedly, a Shakespearean play is more demanding than the average teen novel—but it doesn't have to be boring and it doesn't have to be "dumb."

Here is part of my bag of tricks for teaching a Shakespeare unit so that even my "whip and chair" Grade 10's admit that "there might be something to this Shakespeare guy." Each unit consists of a short introduction, a cartoon version of the play, and a quick quiz. (Quiz answers follow this introduction, beginning on page *vii*.)

Yes, cartoons. Of little animals (dachshunds, to be specific), the only thing I can draw. Okay, you say I'm pandering to the lowest common denominator and I'll reply that I'm in very good, if not exalted, company: Shakespeare used dumb shows and clowns to reach the groundlings. My average Grade 10's are very similar to groundlings—they need to be convinced that the play is worthwhile. (But at least they don't throw rotten vegetables.) The cartoons provide an easy access to the storyline. Also, they are non-threatening; they demystify this "Shakespeare stuff."

I began drawing the cartoons long before I used them in class for a Shakespeare unit. Originally, they were a quick way of telling the story of a Shakespeare play to a class before we went to a production, because students need some help in following the plays' unfamiliar language and complex plot structure. I live in a rural area within reach of a largish city, so I had access to two or three productions a year. Frequently I would want a group of students to see the production but not necessarily study the play in class: perhaps that play wasn't on the curriculum; perhaps the books weren't available because someone else nabbed the set before I did; perhaps I wanted them to see this production as a comparison to a tragedy/comedy/history/romance we were already studying.

Sometimes a production would be done locally, or even come to the schools, and the other teachers or parent supervisors would want to know what it was about before taking their students to see it. The cartoons allowed them to make a decision without having to first slog through the entire play. Failing a live production being available, the cartoons are a useful introduction to a videotape of the play. (I'm a firm believer that a play should be seen—preferably live—as well as read.) Also, because the cartoons use everything from contemporary dress to togas, the students aren't fixated on "doublet and hose" productions.

The rest of the bag of tricks is quite straightforward. The short introduction presents the play's themes in understandable, updated terms. The quick quiz is just ten or twelve questions to make sure the students have understood the bare bones of the plot. The Answer Key offers only my interpretation of the play—one person's view, not necessarily "official" or correct answers. (One of the joys of teaching Shakespeare is a student coming up with another perfectly valid interpretation, an interpretation I hadn't seen at all.)

If we agree that exposing our students to Shakespeare's work is valid, because of the public perception of their importance, the beauty of the language, and the universality of their themes, we should be willing to use everything we have to pry open that oysterlike adolescent mind. We should want more than the castor-oil theory of education (it's good for them). We should want our students to understand and enjoy Shakespeare—even if we have to "go to the dogs" to achieve that!

Answer Key

Quick Quiz 1: *Hamlet*

1. When Hamlet returns from university after his father's death, he discovers that his mother, Gertrude, has married his uncle, Claudius, who has been crowned king.

2. The Ghost tells Hamlet that he was murdered by his brother Claudius. Since Claudius is now the anointed king, the only one who can do anything about righting this awful wrong is the rightful heir, Hamlet.

3. Hamlet knows that ghosts come from Purgatory or Hell and therefore may be evil. This apparition could be a wicked ghost trying to get Hamlet to damn his soul, so Hamlet wants to test Claudius's guilt or innocence for himself.

4. When the wandering players arrive, Hamlet asks them to perform a play which re-enacts the murder. If Claudius doesn't react, then Hamlet knows that the Ghost lied; if Claudius does react, the Ghost told the truth.

5. All three characters must obey Claudius (disobedience is treason) and so they are used to set up situations to test Hamlet's madness—whether they want to or not.

6. Hamlet thinks that the only person who would be behind the curtains in the Queen's bedroom would be Claudius, so he stabs through the curtain without looking.

7. Hamlet begins to get carried away about tormenting Gertrude about her o'erhasty marriage. The Ghost appears to redirect Hamlet to the correct target (Claudius), but it appears only to Hamlet. Gertrude witnesses Hamlet talking to nothing and concludes that he really has gone mad.

8. To have Hamlet tried in Denmark would bring to light too many things that Claudius would rather have hidden. For example, why did Claudius storm out of the play, and what was Polonius doing behind the curtains in the Queen's bedroom? A trial would also give Hamlet a forum and make him the focus of public sympathy.

9. Ophelia can't cope with Hamlet's apparently brutal rejection of her and his senseless murder of her father. She takes refuge in madness.

10. Claudius corrupts Laertes' honorable and natural desire for revenge by getting him to agree to a murder rather than a public trial, and convincing him to use dishonorable means to make sure that the duel ends in Hamlet's death.

11. Hamlet breaks into Rosencrantz and Guildenstern's cabin and finds his death warrant—proof for Gertrude and the rest of Denmark that Claudius lied and conspired against his life.

12. Gertrude drinks the poisoned wine which was intended for Hamlet. Claudius, who knows the wine is lethal, doesn't stop her for fear of being exposed as the poisoner.

13. Laertes witnesses Claudius letting Gertrude drink the poisoned wine, and realizes that Claudius has been lying about his love for Gertrude, among other things. He explains about the poisoned swords and wine. Hamlet forces the rest of the wine down Claudius's throat and then stabs him with the poisoned sword for good measure.

14. Laertes has been stabbed with his own poisoned sword during the duel and dies from it—but he makes his peace with Hamlet first.

15. Hamlet names Fortinbras as his heir so there will be no more dynastic shenanigans. (Besides, Fortinbras is outside with an army!)

Quick Quiz 2: *Julius Caesar*

1. Julius Caesar wants the Senate and people of Rome to crown him king.

2. Cassius opposes Caesar because he is jealous. He comes from the same background as Caesar (social stratum, education, military rank) and doesn't see why Caesar—and not Cassius—is to be crowned.

3. Brutus opposes Caesar because he feels that crowning anyone, even Caesar, is wrong for the country. It will put an end to the Republic that his ancestors fought for.

4. Brutus likes and admires Caesar as a person; Cassius is merely jealous of him. It's Caesar's political ambition to be king that Brutus opposes, but that opposition might entail the destruction of Caesar the person, too.

5. The conspirators (actually Brutus, speaking for the group) allow Antony to speak at Caesar's funeral.

6. Antony sways the crowd by speaking to them on a level they can understand by using short and simple concepts; props such as the "will," the bloodstained toga, and Caesar's dead body; "good ol' boy" modesty; and heavy-handed irony. Before Antony speaks, the crowd wants to crown Brutus (which proves they didn't understand a thing he said!), and after the speech they want to kill Brutus and burn his house.

7. The Triumvirate is a trio of military dictators (Antony, Octavius, and Lepidus) who have taken command of Rome in the wake of the assassination and the riots.

8. Brutus and Cassius are distressed because many innocent people—including Cinna the Poet and Brutus's own wife—have been killed. They feel responsible.

9. The Ghost tells Brutus he will meet him at Philippi.

10. Both Brutus and Cassius commit suicide to avoid the dishonor of being captured, tried, and executed.

Quick Quiz 3: *King Lear*

1. King Lear proposes a contest in which his three daughters will compete in telling him how much they love him; the winner will get the largest chunk of the kingdom.

2. Although Cordelia refuses to take part in Lear's ego-massage and is disinherited, her honesty and integrity win her the hand of the king of France.

3. Edmund plans to get rid of his brother Edgar by convincing their father that Edgar intends patricide.

4. Regan's objection is that Lear is not acting like a retired king. He still commands a huge retinue and wants all the pomp and state of a functioning monarch.

5. The sisters tell Lear that his retinue is too large and unruly: he must cut its numbers dramatically. Lear tries to play the sisters off against each other (you don't love me but Goneril does), but finds the women united against him and in possession of the power that he gave away. He must obey them.

6. The sisters were in Gloucester's house when they confronted Lear and sent him raging into the storm. Gloucester fears that some of the blame must fall to him for this lapse in hospitality—and he does not approve of their actions, anyway.

7. Gloucester disobeys his sovereign's orders by finding Lear in the storm and bringing him to shelter.

8. Regan's husband, Cornwall, puts Gloucester's eyes out with his fingers. A servant forced to witness this is so revolted that he mortally wounds Cornwall, which leaves Regan a widow and free to marry Edmund.

9. Albany's loyalty is to his country. Cordelia is, after all, at the head of a French army.

10. Edmund realizes that if he marries either sister, he will have to kill the other, because neither will submit tamely to the other's winning the ''prize.''

11. Edgar lets Gloucester jump so that he can ''see'' how precious life is, and so Edgar can get out of his ''Poor Tom'' persona.

12. Edmund orders Lear and Cordelia murdered in their cells.

13. Edgar fights as Albany's champion and kills Edmund.

14. Lear has nothing left to live for. He would only have to face a kingdom shattered by his own egoistic stupidity. Besides, he may have died thinking Cordelia was reviving.

15. Kent says he's too old, Albany knows he's not suited to the job by temperament, so Edgar wins the kingship by default.

Quick Quiz 4: *Macbeth*

1. Macbeth has just saved Scotland from revolt from within, led by Macdonwald and the Thane of Cawdor, and invasion from without, led by Sweno, King of Norway.

2. The witches prophesy that Macbeth shall be Thane of Glamis, Thane of Cawdor, and king.

3. The witches prophesy that Banquo will be lesser and greater than Macbeth, not as happy yet happier, and that he will sire kings although he won't be one himself.

4. For Macbeth to become king, the incumbent king must die. Lady Macbeth plans to hurry things along by making sure Duncan dies soon—by murdering him.

5. We know that Banquo suspects the Macbeths of murdering Duncan because he says so in the soliloquy at the beginning of Act III, scene I.

6. Fleance's escape ruins Macbeth's plan because it means that the witches prophecies are still true. Banquo's son may yet rule the kingdom—and for him to rule, Macbeth must be dead. If Macbeth has a son (we're not sure if the Macbeths have any children) the House of Macbeth has to fall for Fleance to rule.

7. Only Macbeth can see Banquo's ghost (but he's also the only one of the company who knows Banquo's dead at this time, too).

8. The apparitions give Macbeth three prophecies: first, a head in a helmet tells him to beware of Macduff; second, a blood-covered baby tells him no man that is born of a woman can harm Macbeth; and third, a crowned child carrying a tree tells him that Macbeth will never be defeated until Birnam Wood comes to Dunsinane Castle.

9. Malcolm is suspicious because his father was killed by someone he trusted, and Macbeth has already sent other people to try to convince Malcolm to come back—into Macbeth's clutches.

10. Macduff never imagined that Macbeth would strike at him by killing his wife, children, and servants. It's not something that an honorable fighting man would ever do.

11. Lady Macbeth has finally realized the full extent of what she and her husband have done, and the guilt of it has driven her mad.

12. The prophecies come true in reverse order: first, Malcolm (the crowned child) orders his men to camouflage their numbers by carrying branches so the wood seems to be moving toward the castle; second, in their final battle, Macduff tells Macbeth that he wasn't born in the conventional sense—he was delivered by Caesarean operation (cut out of his mother's womb); and finally, Macduff brings in Macbeth's head, probably still in its identifiable armor, to prove to all that the tyrant is dead.

Quick Quiz 5: *Measure for Measure*

1. The Duke leaves Angelo and Escalus in charge to avoid being "the heavy" as the laws, long ignored, will be enforced again. In his absence, the people will blame his deputies, even though the enforcement is the Duke's order.

2. The Duke plans to come back in disguise and watch his deputies, for this is a test of whether they will be corrupted by the power he has given to them.

3. Isabella is recalled from her refuge of the nunnery to try to save her brother Claudio's life. He has been arrested and condemned for fornication, and she is to plead for mercy.

4. Angelo offers to trade Isabella's virtue for her brother's life.

5. The Duke has posed as a friar in the prison, where he overhears Isabella explaining to Claudio why she refused Angelo's offer.

6. Mariana agrees to the bed trick because she believes that, because of an earlier marriage contract, she is his wife.

7. Both the Duke and Pompey have arranged extramarital sex. If this is a capital crime for Pompey, shouldn't it be for the Duke as well?

8. Angelo has sexual intercourse with ''Isabella,'' then orders her brother executed anyway—and five hours early.

9. Ragozine, another prisoner, dies of a fever, conveniently providing the necessary head.

10. Isabella doesn't plead very well for things she doesn't believe in, so she'll be more convincing (and grateful later) if she believes that Claudio is dead.

11. Angelo says they're madwomen.

12. Angelo's virtue is publicly exposed as a sham. He's ordered to marry Mariana, then be executed, but Isabella and Mariana plead for his life and the Duke lets him live.

13. The Duke proposes to Isabella. She's speechless.

14. The Duke's directions to the Provost about Lucio's fate are deliberately amibiguous. Lucio could be married, whipped, and hanged, or merely married to Kate Keepdown. The director gets to choose how much justice Lucio will receive. How much does your class think he deserves?

Quick Quiz 6: *A Midsummer Night's Dream*

1. The unfair law is that a father may bury his daughter alive if she doesn't marry the man of his choice.

2. Helena is desperately in love with Demetrius, who is in love with Hermia. In an effort to ingratiate herself with Demetrius, and to prove to him that his love for Hermia is futile, Helena tells him of Hermia's flight to the woods.

3. Because Oberon and Titania have been fighting, all of nature is upset. The crops are failing and the animals are diseased because of the unseasonably rainy weather the fairies have caused.

4. The mechanicals want their play to be a surprise.

5. Oberon enchants Titania so she'll fall in love with the first animate object she sees.

6. Puck doesn't know that there are two Athenian youths loose in the forest, so he puts the love juice on Lysander, who then wakes up and falls madly in love with Helena.

7. Puck has arranged that the first object Titania sees is the "translated" Bottom with his ass's head.

8. Once it's apparent that the lovers have sorted themselves into mutually agreeable pairs, Theseus refuses to let Egeus have his way and bury Hermia alive.

9. The Duke chooses the mechanicals' play over the professional entertainments because he thinks that they have offered it as a wedding present out of affection for him.

10. Aside from missing their cues and forgetting their lines, the mechanicals don't understand the nature of the illusion of theatre. Bottom feels compelled to break out of character to explain to the audience what's going on, for instance.

11. The Duke says that all plays must be helped along by the audience participating with their own imaginations. Some plays need more of this kind of help than others.

12. The fairies bless the three newlywed couples so that their children will be both beautiful and lucky—not a bad wedding present.

Quick Quiz 7: *Othello*

1. Iago hates Cassio because he (not Iago) was promoted, and he hates Othello because Othello did the promoting.

2. Roderigo is in love (or in lust) with Desdemona, and Iago assures him that he will help him obtain her favors.

3. The Turkish fleet is on its way to attack the Venetian Empire. The Duke can't afford to imprison or even offend his ablest general right at this moment.

4. Iago arranges for Cassio, who is a moderate drinker, to get drunk, then creates an incident (with Roderigo's help) which exposes Cassio's dereliction of duty in being drunk when he should be on guard.

5. Desdemona is too naive to realize that pleading for favors for a handsome young man might be misinterpreted by her new husband.

6. Othello takes Cassio's possession of the embroidered handkerchief as proof of Desdemona's infidelity. It was his first gift to her, and Othello assumes that she would not have given it away casually—and not if she still loved him.

7. Roderigo becomes a liability when he begins to question whether all of the jewelry he has given to Iago to give to Desdemona has actually been delivered.

8. Cassio fights back with more skill than Iago expects from a "theoretician" and fights Roderigo off. Iago is interrupted before he can kill Cassio.

9. Desdemona orders the wedding sheets put on the bed and sings the dirge-like "Willow" song.

10. Emilia is the only one (besides Iago) who knows how Cassio must have come into possession of the handkerchief—she found it and gave it to her husband, Iago. Now that she sees that her obedience to her husband has cost her mistress her life, she tells about the handkerchief—and Iago kills her.

11. Roderigo has the last laugh on Iago when the letter detailing his dealings with Iago is found on his dead body.

12. Othello salvages some honor by pronouncing himself one who loved "not wisely but too well" and committing suicide to atone for Desdemona's death.

Quick Quiz 8: *Romeo and Juliet*

1. The Prince says that the next brawl between the feuding families will be punished by death.

2. Romeo's love for Rosaline disintegrates at the sight of Juliet.

3. Romeo and Juliet don't learn that they're from the rival houses of Montague and Capulet until they're already in love.

4. Friar Laurence thinks that presenting the heads of the rival houses with their only son and only daughter married will force them to end the feud.

5. Tybalt kills Mercutio in a fight, which prompts Romeo to kill Tybalt in a duel.

6. He thinks she is mourning her cousin Tybalt, and plans to take her mind off his death by arranging her marriage to Paris within two days.

7. Friar Laurence cannot marry Juliet and Paris, because he knows that she is already married to Romeo. Juliet also threatens suicide, which would condemn her soul. The catatonic drug offers a third solution.

8. The Friar's messenger is held up so that Romeo never gets the Friar's letter and assumes that Juliet really is dead.

9. Paris tries to arrest Romeo because he thinks Romeo intends to vandalize the Capulet's tomb.

10. Friar Laurence, who should have offered Juliet spiritual comfort in her hour of need, runs out on her (literally) when he hears the watch (police) coming to the tomb. His desertion gives her the opportunity to commit suicide.

11. They find the dead bodies of Romeo and Juliet.

12. The Montagues and Capulets bury the feud when they bury their only children.

Quick Quiz 9: *The Taming of the Shrew*

1. Baptista is holding Bianca as ransom (or bait) so that her suitors will arrange a marriage for her older sister, Kate.

2. Lucentio disguises himself as a tutor—the only man allowed near Bianca at the moment.

3. Petruchio is interested in Katharina because she is wealthy and will have no rival suitors to compete with.

4. Hortensio decides to get closer to Bianca by disguising himself as a tutor. (Great minds think alike . . . .)

5. In both her wooing and wedding, Kate is a very unwilling participant.

6. Petruchio "kills Kate with kindness"—and gives her a taste of her own behavior—by being so overly solicitous that Kate gets no sleep, nothing to eat, and nothing new to wear.

7. Tranio hires the pedant to play "his" father because Baptista is demanding assurances about the financial security of Bianca's suitors. Lucentio (who is being played by Tranio so Lucentio can play the tutor) must produce a father to close the deal for Bianca. Notice that Baptista required no such assurances for Kate.

8. When Lucentio's father sees his son's servant masquerading as his son and the pedant as the father, he assumes that they have murdered Lucentio.

9. Lucentio marries Bianca, Hortensio marries the widow, and Kate and Petruchio celebrate their wedding.

10. Kate is the only wife who obeys the order.

Quick Quiz 10: *The Tempest*

1. Prospero has created the storm to shipwreck the people on the island so they will be in his power.

2. Ariel and Caliban are two natives of the island. Ariel is a spirit of air and fire, capable of being controlled by threats and able to do magical transmutations. Caliban is a more earthy being who must be controlled by corporal punishment; he provides the necessities of life for Prospero and Miranda.

3. Miranda's reaction to Ferdinand is love at first sight—as his reaction is to her. Prospero arrests Ferdinand to put some obstacles in the way of their love, both to test Ferdinand's mettle and to make him earn Miranda so that he will value her more highly.

4. Antonio and Sebastian attempt to murder Alonso and Gonzalo so that Sebastian can be king of Naples—not that being king matters all that much when one is lost on a desert island.

5. Caliban worships Stephano because Stephano gives him liquor. Caliban has no perspective from which to judge the worth of the drunken butler over the humanist scholar; in fact, he wants Stephano to murder Prospero.

6. Gonzalo doesn't see the harpy because he has no guilt—he treated Prospero and Miranda as honorably as he was able.

7. The wedding masque is interrupted by the murderous drunks, now reeking from their ducking in the cesspool. The drunks are diverted from their plan by the "glistening apparel" and then chased out of the way by dogs.

8. Prospero now has each character in his power. Then Ariel tells him that Gonzalo is crying for Alonso's plight. If a man as honorable as Gonzalo weeps for Alonso, then Alonso must have qualities that Prospero doesn't know about. If Prospero is going to play God, he had better be omniscient. If he is punishing Antonio and Alonso only to return pain, he is no better than they are. He decides not to punish, but to forgive.

9. Alonso tried to have Miranda killed for Prospero's "crime." Instead of punishing the son for the father's crime, Prospero gives Alonso back his son, whom he thought drowned.

10. Prospero now loses Miranda to Ferdinand because her husband, not her father, will be the most important person in her life.

11. When Caliban sees Prospero in his proper ducal robes, he realizes the importance and nobility of the man—especially in comparison to Stephano.

12. Prospero asks the audience to applaud.

Quick Quiz 11: *Twelfth Night*

1. Olivia is probably trying to tell the Duke (politely because he is her lord) that she is not interested in his suit.

2. Viola, a lady of gentle birth, has no one to protect her and nowhere to go, now that Olivia is not receiving guests because of her "mourning." At the rate Viola is giving money away she will soon be penniless. She needs a job but has no practical skills.

3. Viola solves her problem by dressing up as a gentleman-in-waiting upon the Duke. This plan backfires when Olivia takes a fancy to the young "gentleman."

4. Malvolio tells Sir Toby, Sir Andrew, and Feste to be quiet when they're having a party in Olivia's house. When he can't make the relative, the guest, and the favored fool be quiet, he turns on Maria and humiliates her by reminding her of her employee status. The partiers decide to retaliate by setting up a situation which will humiliate Malvolio.

5. The letter asks Malvolio to smile, to speak of matters above his station, to be unkind (unkinder?) to servants, and to wear yellow stockings cross-gartered.

6. Malvolio is so conceited that he never considers that the letter could be a practical joke. In his mind it's entirely reasonable that Olivia should fall madly in love with him.

7. Sir Toby has an unkind sense of humor: it amuses him to see people put into uncomfortable situations. Besides, this situation will distract Sir Andrew from leaving.

8. Antonio is arrested when he intervenes in the duel because he is a wanted man in Illyria. Several years before he had fought against the Duke in a sea battle.

9. Sebastian is pleasantly surprised to meet a beautiful and wealthy woman who thinks she knows him quite well.

10. Feste plays a dimwitted priest who tries to get Malvolio to agree to obviously stupid ideas to get out of prison. Then he returns as himself and is "surprised" by Malvolio's plight.

11. Instead of being happy that two people he cares for have found happiness, the Duke punishes them by banishing them from Illyria.

12. Sebastian's sudden entrance makes it clear that there are two "Cesarios"—only one of whom Olivia has married.

13. Once the Duke realizes that Cesario/Viola is a woman, he remembers his pontificating about love when he couldn't see it right under his nose, and realizes how foolish he must have sounded.

14. Malvolio is humiliated and his pretentions exposed in front of anybody who is anybody in Illyria.

15. Sir Toby has married Maria.

Quick Quiz 12: *The Winter's Tale*

1. Leontes and Polixenes have been friends since childhood.

2. Leontes can't get Polixenes to stay any longer, but Hermione can.

3. Leontes orders Camillo to murder Polixenes. If Camillo disobeys the order he's a traitor to his king; if he obeys it, especially knowing that Polixenes is innocent, he's a murderer.

4. First Leontes orders the baby burned alive, then decides that abandoning her on the seacoast of Polixenes' country is more appropriate.

5. Leontes expects that the Oracle will agree with him—that Hermione is guilty of adultery.

6. Immediately after Leontes proves that he is a tyrant by refusing to accept even religious authority, he hears of the deaths of Hermione and his son Mamillius. He realizes his error but it's too late. His baby daughter is now lost, too.

7. The Old Shepherd is a decent man. He doesn't feel that a baby should have to die for the sins of her parents, so he decides to adopt Perdita before his judgment is influenced by the gold.

8. Polixenes is angry that Florizel has promised to marry Perdita. As prince, Florizel should marry for state reasons, not love.

9. It's not Perdita's fault that Florizel (who she didn't even know was the prince) has fallen in love with her and defied his father. Again, she is being punished for someone else's "sins."

10. Camillo is homesick for Sicilia, and he has seen where hasty decisions like Polixenes' can lead.

11. The fardel contains the things found with Perdita as a baby: her wrapper, embroidered by Hermione's ladies; the gold; and a letter in Antigonus's handwriting saying who she is. Since neither shepherd can read, they don't know what the letter contains—evidence that "the lost is found."

12. Would you want to live with a man who was responsible for the death of your son, who unjustly accused and imprisoned you and put you through a shameful public trial, then ordered your baby daughter burnt? Hermione has probably been living in seclusion until she was sure that Leontes had truly repented and learned not to give in to his impulses. Or the gods could have brought the statue to life to make the story end happily.

Hamlet

Hamlet

Introduction

What do you do when your mother marries someone you distrust and dislike?

What do you do when someone very dear to you asks you to do something important, and you're not sure if that person is telling the truth?

What do you do when you're faced with a situation in which you must hurt the people you love now to spare them more hurt later?

Hamlet is a long, complicated, and demanding play, but it speaks to teenagers because Hamlet's dilemmas are the dilemmas of indecision and powerlessness, two conditions that teenagers identify with. Hamlet's mother remarries someone who takes Hamlet's place both in her affections and in the political structure; his girlfriend acts inexplicably; his father tells him to do something he really doesn't want to do. No wonder teenagers understand what makes Hamlet tick; despite his age, he's one of them.

Hamlet

1. The play begins with guards and a young courtier nervously assembled on the castle battlements. The reason for their vigil appears—a ghost. In fact, it is the ghost of the dead king, Hamlet, but it will not speak to them.

2. Prince Hamlet, the ghost's son, is in the court below, ostentatiously wearing mourning black amid everyone else's bright colors. (The court is celebrating the marriage of his mother, Gertrude, to his uncle, Claudius, barely a month after King Hamlet's death.)

Gloom

3. Hamlet is angry, humiliated, and physically revolted by the thought of the marriage. He makes unkind comments and speaks unconvincingly of suicide: he is feeling very sorry for himself.

LIKE THIS   MY DAD?

4. The young man on the battlements, Hamlet's good friend Horatio, tells the Prince what he and the men have seen. Since unquiet ghosts often foretell disasters, they decide they had better find out what the ghost means.

TAKE CARE, LITTLE SISTER

5. Laertes, a contemporary of Hamlet's, is going back to university. He says farewell to his sister Ophelia and warns her of her fondness for Hamlet. The Prince, he says, cannot marry for love; even if he loves Ophelia, she had better be careful.

-SEDUCTION!

6. Laertes is sent off by his father, Polonius, with an earful of advice. Polonius talks to Ophelia about Hamlet, but his interpretation is that Hamlet will say anything to seduce a girl. (Polonius would.) He forbids Ophelia to see Hamlet and tells her to send back all gifts.

Hamlet

7. Hamlet, Horatio, and the guards wait on the windy walls of Elsinore. All are nervous—especially Hamlet. The ghost appears and beckons Hamlet to the most dangerous part of the walls. Though the others try to prevent him (the ghost may be a demon), Hamlet follows.

8. The ghost tells Hamlet the news that he didn't want to hear: Uncle Claudius murdered Hamlet's father, King Hamlet, and seduced Gertrude into marrying him. Hamlet now must avenge his father's murder, but leave his mother to heaven. The ghost vanishes.

9. Hamlet realizes the news puts him and his friends in danger. He swears them to secrecy (with the help of the ghost) but he really doesn't want to be the avenger of his father. He doesn't know what to do.

10. Ophelia reports to her father, Polonius: she is very disturbed by Hamlet's strange behavior (as are Gertrude and Claudius). Hamlet, his clothing all messy, has come into her room and just stared at her.

11. Claudius has summoned two of Hamlet's university friends, Rosencrantz and Guildenstern, to spy on Hamlet. They agree to this quite willingly (although they don't have much choice: Claudius is the king).

12. Polonius bustles in, saying he's found the cause of Hamlet's madness—love. He whips out one of Ophelia's letters from Hamlet and reads it before the entire court (sensitive, isn't he?). He criticizes its style and says he'll set up a meeting others can watch.

Shakespeare Made Easy

13. The rest of the court clears out as Hamlet approaches. Polonius tries to get him to commit himself about Ophelia, but Hamlet weaves a web of half-mad words that confounds the old man.

14. When Rosencrantz and Guildenstern try to pump Hamlet for information, the result is much the same. Hamlet finds out they are working for Claudius and warns them they're playing a dangerous game.

15. Hamlet is diverted by the arrival of traveling players. He begins a speech he liked, and the players' leader finishes it for him, speaking so passionately that he changes color and cries. Hamlet engages the troup to play "The Mousetrap" before the court tomorrow night.

16. Alone, Hamlet berates himself. If the player can work up that much emotion about a literary character, why can't Hamlet do something about his father's murder? The play will test Claudius; if he reacts, he's guilty (the play is similar to the murder); if he doesn't, the ghost is an evil spirit.

17. Remember Polonius's plan for Ophelia? He plants her in the hall to meet Hamlet while he and Claudius eavesdrop from behind tapestries. Hamlet realizes this is a setup. He tells Ophelia to get to a nunnery (i.e., to a safe place) before the court corrupts her, and threatens Claudius.

18. Angered at Hamlet's implied threat, Claudius decides to send Hamlet away to England. Polonius suggests that Gertrude might be able to reach Hamlet where Ophelia failed.

     Shakespeare Made Easy

Hamlet

19. Hamlet tells the players how to act, then, as the court assembles to hear the play, he is *very* rude to Ophelia. Since she hasn't left, he assumes she is being used willingly. Poor Ophelia is even more distressed and confused by his behavior.

20. The play begins and the players act out a king being murdered (just the way King Hamlet was) by a trusted advisor, who then woos and wins the widowed queen. Gertrude watches calmly.

21. But not Claudius! He gets up and storms out before the play is finished. Now he knows that Hamlet knows that his father's death was murder, how it was done, and "who done it." Suddenly Hamlet is a very real danger to Claudius.

22. Hamlet is delighted at how his plan worked. He now knows that Claudius is guilty and the ghost was real. Again he warns Rosencrantz and Guildenstern that they can't manipulate him. Although he sees through Polonius's fawning, he agrees to visit Gertrude.

23. Now that he knows he's in danger, Claudius tries to pray. He won't give up his ill-gotten prizes, so he just kneels and recites formulas of prayer. Hamlet sees him, alone and unguarded, but believes that to kill Claudius while he's praying would send him to heaven. Hamlet tiptoes on by.

24. Polonius has hidden behind the big tapestry in Gertrude's bedroom. When Hamlet begins to get angry at Gertrude, Polonius calls for help. Thinking the voice comes from Claudius, Hamlet stabs right through the tapestry and kills Polonius. Gertrude is horrified.

 Shakespeare Made Easy

25. As Hamlet tries to convince Gertrude to leave Claudius (without telling her that her present husband murdered her former husband), King Hamlet's ghost appears to protect Gertrude. She cannot see it, and as Hamlet talks to "nothing," she becomes convinced he really is mad.

26. Hamlet's murder of Polonius is discovered, and Hamlet is arrested. Hamlet is rude to Claudius, but Claudius won't react. (He doesn't want to put Hamlet on trial; Hamlet knows too much.) Instead, Claudius breaks his own land's laws by sending Hamlet away to England.

27. On his way, Hamlet meets a captain in Fortinbras's army. Fortinbras, the Prince of Norway, is held up as the ideal, but Hamlet wonders about the war he's waging for a scrap of land that can't bury the bodies of the men who will die fighting for it. If that's honor, why, Hamlet wonders, does he worry about killing one man?

28. Back at the castle, Ophelia has gone mad. The man she loves has rejected her privately and publicly and killed her father. She wanders about the castle, singing songs about dead men and faithless lovers.

29. Laertes bursts into the castle at the head of a mob. Claudius, playing the king, dares them to touch his sacred person. Laertes dismisses his followers and demands to know what happened to his father and why Hamlet has not been punished.

30. As Claudius says he's not responsible, Ophelia comes back in. Laertes is horrified at what has happened to his beloved sister and vows vengeance. Like Hamlet, he is now a young man with a mission.

Hamlet

31. Sailors have brought Horatio a letter. In it he finds that Hamlet was captured by pirates when he led the attack on them. (To die in battle would be the easy way out for Hamlet, the reluctant avenger.) Hamlet is on his way home to Denmark.

32. Claudius is working on Laertes, turning Laertes' geniune vengeance into a tool of a corrupt king. Laertes agrees to Claudius's scheme of a duel with trick swords and poisoned wine, and suggests poisoning the tip of his sword as well. Claudius has corrupted him.

33. Laertes and Claudius have received Hamlet's letter saying he's returning and vow to act quickly. Gertrude brings news of Ophelia's death—suicide by drowning. She is upset, Laertes is devastated, but Claudius is only annoyed at the inconvenience.

34. Two gravediggers work on Ophelia's grave and discuss the case. Suicides weren't buried in churchyards, and both these men know that if Ophelia hadn't been who she was, she wouldn't be buried here. (Claudius is now bending church law.) Hamlet and Horatio approach.

35. Hamlet plays with the idea of death, which is never far from his mind. He speculates on death in general, but then the gravedigger makes it personal by handing him the skull of a childhood friend, Yorick the jester. Hamlet has scarcely recovered himself when a funeral approaches.

36. Hamlet does not know Ophelia is dead, but as he spies on the funeral the awful truth dawns on him. Laertes, Gertrude, and Claudius all mourn Ophelia in her shabby little funeral.

Shakespeare Made Easy

37. When Laertes, wild with grief, leaps into Ophelia's grave, Hamlet can stand being hidden no longer. He comes out and gets into an unfortunate fight with Laertes about who loved Ophelia most.

38. Later, a much calmer Hamlet tells Horatio what he's done. He has stolen the letter his escorts (Rosencrantz and Guildenstern) were carrying, which commanded the King of England to execute Hamlet immediately, and replaced it with a letter that says "execute bearers."

39. Horatio is aghast that Hamlet would order the deaths of his university chums. Hamlet says they were willing tools of Claudius and he is not concerned. Besides, now he has hard evidence (the letter) of Claudius's plotting to show the court, the courts, and Gertrude.

40. Osric, a foppish young courtier, delivers a challenge. The king has bet six Arab horses against six French swords that Hamlet can beat Laertes in a duel. After playing with Osric a bit, Hamlet accepts the challenge.

41. Horatio is worried and fears another plot by Claudius. Hamlet says the key to life is to live it as though every day would be your last and that he is ready for what is to come.

42. Before the duel begins, Claudius drops a pearl coated with poison into a goblet of wine as a toast to Hamlet. Hamlet apologizes to Laertes for his behavior, saying they're in similar circumstances. Laertes begins to have second thoughts.

Hamlet

43. Hamlet wins the first two touches of the sword. Gertrude is so pleased at his performance and apparent sanity that she takes the poisoned cup and drinks a toast to him. Claudius doesn't stop her (because he'd have to explain why).

44. Laertes, shocked that the king would let Gertrude (whom he claims to love so much) drink the poisoned wine, continues the duel. He wounds Hamlet with his poisoned sword, but in the fray the swords are exchanged and he is wounded with it, too.

45. Suddenly Gertrude cries out that the wine was poisoned. Claudius tries to deny it, but Laertes, seeing him for what he really is, tells the whole plot—poisoned wine, poisoned swords, and all.

46. Hamlet turns on Claudius, forces the last of the poisoned wine down his throat and stabs him with the venomed sword for good measure.

47. Realizing he is dying, Hamlet forgives Laertes (who, because he has been stabbed closer to the heart, dies first). He gives the kingdom to Fortinbras. Then he dies in Horatio's arms.

48. Fortinbras returns from his Polish war at that moment and is horrified by all the dead bodies in the court. He is sorry Hamlet is dead, for he feels Hamlet would have ruled well. He takes over and orders the honor of a state funeral for the dead prince.

Shakespeare Made Easy

Name: _____ Date: _____

Hamlet: Quick Quiz

1. What problem confronts Hamlet when he returns home for his father's funeral?
   _____
   _____

2. How does what the Ghost tells him change his life? _____
   _____

3. Why doesn't he act on the Ghost's information immediately? _____
   _____

4. What is Hamlet's plan? _____
   _____

5. How are Rosencrantz, Guildenstern, and Ophelia used against Hamlet? _____
   _____

6. Why does Hamlet kill Polonius? _____
   _____

7. What convinces Gertrude that Hamlet is mad? _____
   _____

8. Why is Hamlet sent to England rather than tried for Polonius's murder in
   Denmark? _____
   _____

9. What happens to Ophelia? _____
   _____

10. How does Claudius corrupt Laertes? _____
    _____

11. What "hard evidence" does Hamlet find against Claudius? _____
    _____

12. How does Gertrude die? _____
    _____

13. How does Claudius die? _____
    _____

14. How does Laertes die? _____
    _____

15. What does Hamlet do before he dies? _____
    _____

Julius Caesar

Julius Caesar

Introduction

What do you do when someone you love or admire is going to do something which you feel is very wrong and will hurt other people?

Are you justified in doing something wrong to prevent another from doing something you feel is even more wrong?

These are the central questions of *Julius Caesar*. They are questions which are just as valid today as they were in Shakespeare's, or even Caesar's time. The play is not so much about the political situation in the Roman Empire as it is about the moral conflicts of its central character, and those moral conflicts are similar to the ones teenagers face today. Instead of your beloved father image changing the political structure of Rome, imagine that your older brother, whom you idolize, is dealing drugs in an elementary school playground, or that your sports idol is taking steroids and is likely to get caught . . . .

Julius Caesar

1. The play begins as two senators confront a group of drunken plebeians (commoners) who are celebrating Julius Caesar's victory over rival general Pompey. The senators are upset that the plebeians are rejoicing over a Roman killing a Roman.

2. We meet Julius Caesar as he embarrasses his wife in public by telling his right-hand man to touch her during the rites of Lupercal so she'll have a child. A soothsayer tells him to "beware the ides of March."

3. While Caesar and his followers go off to see the race of Lupercal, Brutus remains behind. Cassius, his brother-in-law, remains behind also. He wants to talk to Brutus, in private.

4. Cassius realizes Brutus is worried about Caesar's growing power and tries to get Brutus to commit himself to opposing Caesar. Cassius is jealous of Caesar.

5. Caesar and his party come back. Caesar looks upset but can immediately tell Cassius is up to something. He warns Antony about Cassius's "lean and hungry look."

6. Brutus and Cassius ask Casca to tell them what upset Caesar. Casca describes how Antony offered Caesar a crown and how the crowd's reactions made him refuse it (regretfully, Casca thinks).

Julius Caesar

7. Brutus leaves without committing himself to anything. Cassius plans to forge letters to Brutus to make it seem that many Romans oppose Caesar and are looking for a leader. (Cassius will try anything to get Brutus into his conspiracy.)

8. It's a month later, the eve of the ides of March. A violent storm terrifies Casca. Cassius uses Casca's fear to get him to join the conspiracy by telling him the storm is because Julius Caesar is to be crowned tomorrow. Casca joins.

9. Brutus walks alone in his garden. He has to make up his mind tonight about killing his friend. He loves Caesar as a person but hates his lust for power. No man, he decides, can handle all that power.

10. The conspirators call on Brutus. Cassius is so anxious to have Brutus as "front man" that he makes three concessions: they won't swear an oath of loyalty; they won't ask Cicero to join; and they won't kill Antony, too. Brutus joins.

11. When the conspirators have left, Portia, Brutus's wife, emerges from her hiding place. She demands to know what her husband is up to, saying she can keep a secret. (She's stabbed herself in the thigh to prove it.) Brutus apologizes, but before he can explain, a last person calls.

12. Now we see why Cassius wanted Brutus to head the conspiracy. The visitor, Ligarius, doesn't really care about the details; it's enough for him to know that Brutus thinks the conspiracy is right. He joins.

Shakespeare Made Easy

13. At Caesar's house, Caesar is awake because of the storm. His wife is worried, and tells, asks, then begs him not to go to the Senate today. Finally (because Caesar is nervous himself) he agrees.

14. Decius, one of the conspirators, arrives to get Caesar to the Senate. He hears Caesar is not going because of Calpurnia's awful dream (of a statue of Caesar spouting blood) and reinterprets it as a fortunate dream. Besides, he adds, the Senate had planned to crown Caesar . . . .

15. As Caesar arrives at the Senate, Artemidorus tries to pass him a scroll which warns Caesar of the conspiracy, but Caesar won't take it. The soothsayer reminds him that today is the ides of March.

16. Another senator wishes the conspirators luck. (They haven't been as secret as they'd thought.) The conspirators, including Brutus, surround Caesar and stab him.

17. Mortally wounded, Caesar turns to see Brutus with a dagger. He says, "Et tu, Brute!" (You too, Brutus!) "Then, fall, Caesar!" Then he dies at the base of Pompey's statue.

18. Immediately there is panic, but Brutus and Cassius assure the terrified senators no one else is to be killed. Then the conspirators bathe their hands in Caesar's blood to show they are proud of their deed.

Julius Caesar

19. Antony, who has been decoyed by a conspirator, returns and sees Caesar's body. He tells the group that if they're going to kill him, they should do it now. Brutus says they're not.

20. Antony agrees to go along with the conspirators as long as they can explain why they killed Caesar. Also, he wants to speak at Caesar's funeral. Brutus agrees and Antony shakes all the conspirators' bloody hands. (Cassius doesn't like this a bit.)

21. As soon as the conspirators have left, Antony turns to Caesar's body and apologizes. He swears he will avenge Caesar's death. A servant brings news that Caesar's nephew Octavius is a few miles out of Rome, with an army. Antony smiles.

22. Outside the crowd gathers. Brutus makes a complicated "arty" speech which the plebeians don't understand. He says he slew Caesar because kingship is too much power for any man. The plebeians want to crown Brutus.

23. Then Antony comes in with Caesar's body. The crowd is hostile, but soon begins to be swayed by his understandable style and his hinting that Caesar has left them something in his will.

24. Antony plays the crowd like a violin. He cries, shows them Caesar's cut and bloody toga, telling them who stabbed where (how does he know?), and then shows them Caesar's body. Finally he reads the will. The crowd riots.

Shakespeare Made Easy

25. A victim of the riot is Cinna the Poet, who is torn to pieces because of his name (and because he's in the wrong place at the wrong time). The riots give Antony an excuse to bring in Octavius's army and declare martial law. Brutus and Cassius flee.

26. Rome is now controlled by Antony, Octavius, and Lepidus, who make a "hit list" of people they intend to kill. Soon Lepidus himself may be on it, for Octavius and Antony already plan to get rid of him.

27. In a camp in Sardis, Brutus awaits the arrival of Cassius. Both have raised armies to fight Antony and Octavius, but there is a dispute between them.

28. Inside where the troops cannot see, the argument erupts into full spate. The two commanders argue about how Cassius raises money, who is the better soldier, etc., until Cassius comes out with what's really bothering him.

29. "Even when you killed Caesar, you liked him better than you like me," Cassius cries. Suddenly Brutus's anger evaporates and both men turn and laugh at the poet the men have sent in to calm them.

30. As the two friends talk, we hear of the awful conditions in Rome. A hundred senators have died and Portia has committed suicide. Cassius feels awful.

Julius Caesar

31. Cassius wants the army to stay put, but he gives in to Brutus, who wants to meet Antony and Octavius halfway, at Philippi. Later Caesar's ghost appears to Brutus and says, "Thou shalt see me at Philippi," but Brutus goes anyway. Perhaps he wants to die there.

32. Before the fighting, the leaders of the two armies meet. Antony and Octavius are obviously disagreeing (but agree there will be no treaty). Brutus and Cassius say goodbye to each other: they don't expect to win.

33. Brutus lets his troops go too soon. Cassius, cut off, thinks they have lost because Pindarus, his servant, misinterprets what he sees. (Remember, *everyone* is in Roman uniform.) Rather than be captured, Cassius commits suicide.

34. Titinius, Cassius's friend, comes back with a wreath of victory for him. Seeing him dead, he too commits suicide. Brutus interprets this as Caesar avenging himself, and orders another attack.

35. The attack fails and the battle is lost. While a couple of his brave officers buy Brutus time, Brutus orders his servant to hold his sword, then runs onto it, killing himself.

36. When Brutus's body is discovered, Antony calls him "the noblest Roman of them all" because only Brutus acted for the good of the state alone, not from personal motives. They take his body for honorable burial.

Name: _____   Date: _____

Julius Caesar: **Quick Quiz**

1. What does Julius Caesar want the Senate and people of Rome to do? _____
   _____
   _____

2. Why does Cassius oppose Caesar? _____
   _____

3. Why does Brutus oppose Caesar? _____
   _____

4. Why is Brutus's decision more troublesome than Cassius's? _____
   _____

5. What mistake do the conspirators make (besides not assassinating Antony along with Caesar)? _____
   _____
   _____

6. How does Antony change the crowd's feelings about the assassination of Caesar?
   _____
   _____

7. What is the Triumvirate? _____
   _____
   _____

8. Why are Brutus and Cassius distressed by what's going on in Rome? _____
   _____

9. What does the Ghost say to Brutus? _____
   _____

10. What happens to Brutus and Cassius at the end of the battle? _____
    _____

King Lear

King Lear

Introduction

What would you do if your father asked you and the rest of your family to say how much you loved him as a way of deciding who gets what in his will?

How would you cope with someone who wants all the rights of a position but wants you to do all the work?

When do you decide that a parent is too senile to be treated like a normal adult?

These are the questions facing Lear's daughters in *King Lear*. Lear plans to give away his kingdom, yet still remain its king. The differing ways that his daughters handle his "gift" and its consequences are the stuff of the play. Cordelia refuses to beg; Goneril and Regan refuse to be eternally beholden to their father. Eventually Lear's gift destroys them all. Would your family handle such a crisis any better?

King Lear

1. As the Earl of Kent and the Earl of Gloucester wait for the king, Gloucester proudly introduces his illegitimate son Edmund, noting that he also has an older, legitimate son, Edgar.

2. When the king arrives he, too, is preoccupied with his heirs. He unrolls a map of England and declares his intention to divide his kingdom and retire. He asks his eldest daughter to tell how much she loves him.

3. Goneril waxes poetic about how much she loves her father, and so in turn does her sister Regan. Pleased and flattered, Lear awards each a third of his kingdom.

4. Cordelia, the youngest daughter, is next. She says she loves her father as much as she ought, for when she marries she must love her husband, too. (The other sisters have sworn that their only love is their father.)

5. Furious at what seems a public "slap in the face" from his cherished youngest daughter, Lear refuses to give her anything—including a dowry. He divides the kingdom between Goneril and Regan.

6. The Earl of Kent speaks on Cordelia's behalf, saying that Cordelia loves her father and that Lear's action is rash, if not mad. Lear banishes him on pain of death and dismemberment.

7. King Lear then calls forth Cordelia's suitors, the Duke of Burgundy and the King of France. When they discover that she now has no dowry, the duke bows out but the king is delighted to marry her. They leave.

8. Regan and Goneril are pleased with what's happened, but agree that Lear loved Cordelia best and could change his mind again.

9. Edmund, Gloucester's illegitimate son, plans to steal his legitimate brother's inheritance. He's prepared a letter which he cons his father into reading, in which "Edgar" proposes Gloucester's death and splitting the estate.

10. Edmund defends Edgar, saying he wrote the letter to test him, and didn't really mean it. Naturally Gloucester is upset. The world, he says, is upset, with eclipses and rash acts, such as Kent's banishment.

11. Alone, Edmund is delighted with his plot. When he meets Edgar he steers the conversation to eclipses and other "unnaturalnesses" like the sudden anger of Gloucester against Edgar. He warns Edgar to carry a dagger.

12. Meanwhile, at Goneril's, King Lear is proving a difficult guest, for although he has retired, he still insists on being treated like a king. Goneril decides to consult Regan about what to do about the old man.

Shakespeare Made Easy

13. The banished Earl of Kent, now in disguise, applies to Lear and is taken into his service just in time to see Goneril's new treatment of her father. Her steward, Oswald, as directed, is deliberately rude.

14. Angered, Lear calls for his Fool, but the Fool offers little amusement. He calls Lear a fool for giving away all his titles but "fool." (Kent agrees.) He calls Lear "Lear's Shadow."

15. Goneril complains to her father that his followers—a hundred of them—disrupt her court. Lear is so angry that he threatens to go and live with Regan. He curses Goneril and calls her thankless.

16. While Lear listens to the Fool's foolery and hopes he isn't going mad, he sends Kent ahead with letters for the Earl of Gloucester. But Goneril has also sent Oswald with letters to Regan.

17. Edmund is still scheming against his brother. He convinces Edgar to run away, wounds himself, then tells Gloucester that Edgar tried to kill him. Gloucester believes him and orders Edgar arrested.

18. Oswald arrives with letters for Regan only to find his way blocked by Kent, who picks a fight. No one recognizes the "king's messenger" and he is put in the stocks, but Gloucester doesn't like that.

King Lear

19. When Lear arrives at his other daughter's court, he discovers his messenger in the stocks. Kent warns Lear that Goneril has written to Regan—although his account is not exactly what the audience saw happen.

20. At first Regan and her husband, the Duke of Cornwall, won't see Lear. Then Regan refuses to listen to Lear's rantings about Goneril's ingratitude and how he regrets giving her half his kingdom.

21. Goneril arrives and the sisters present a united front against Lear. Regan asks him to go back to Goneril's and dismiss fifty of his attendants—or stay with Regan and have only twenty-five knights.

22. Suddenly Goneril's allowing fifty knights looks better, but when Lear says he'll return to Goneril's, she asks why he needs any knights when she has servants. Lear, aghast, blunders into the storm as others seek shelter.

23. Kent realizes that the husbands of Goneril and Regan might fight to see who gets all of the kingdom. He sends a messenger to the secret French camp to tell Cordelia how her father is being treated.

24. Kent finds Lear, attended now only by his loyal Fool, wandering about in the storm. Kent tries to get them to shelter and Lear, out of concern for the Fool, agrees.

25. Gloucester confides to Edmund that he didn't like the way Regan and her husband treated Lear—giving Edmund information to buy their favor with.

26. Lear, discovering that ex-kings get cold like other men, takes shelter in the hovel where he, Kent, and the Fool meet Edgar, who has disguised himself as a wandering lunatic. Poor Tom.

27. As the group listens to Tom's ravings, Gloucester arrives. Although he has been ordered to leave them out in the storm, he cannot. He takes all—even his unrecognized son—back to his house.

28. The Duke of Cornwall is furious with Gloucester's actions. Edmund agrees and supplies another letter (another forgery) which says that Gloucester is allied with the French, who are at Dover. Edmund is named Duke of Gloucester.

29. The strain has made Lear lose his wits. Lear, Tom, and the Fool put on a mock trial, using furniture (joint-stools) as stand-ins for Goneril and Regan. Kent, brokenhearted, looks on. Gloucester tells him to take Lear to Dover.

30. Gloucester, having gotten Lear away to safety, is arrested. Regan, Goneril, and the Duke of Cornwall interrogate him. They put out one of his eyes.

31. A servant cannot stand this. He attacks and wounds Cornwall, but is killed by Regan. Cornwall puts Gloucester's other eye out and tells about Edmund. Only now that he is blind does Gloucester see the truth about Edgar.

32. Gloucester, blinded, is thrown out onto the heath where he stumbles upon Poor Tom (Edgar). Edgar is horrified, but maintains his disguise and leads Gloucester toward Dover.

33. Goneril rides home to rouse Albany, her "mild husband," to raise troops against the French at Dover, only to find that the worm has turned. The duke cannot stand what has been done to Lear—then he hears about Gloucester!

34. Kent arrives in the French camp to find Cordelia in charge because her husband had to return home. She is horrified at what her sisters have done and the effect it has had upon her father.

35. Goneril has sent Edmund a letter and Regan wants to know why. Now that her husband has died of the wound the servant gave him, she has designs on Edmund herself . . . .

36. Gloucester has had "Tom" take him to a cliff where he can throw himself over, and Edgar lets him think he's fallen and been miraculously preserved. Even blind, Gloucester may be luckier than Lear.

Shakespeare Made Easy

37. Lear is now completely mad. He wanders around babbling, decked out in wildflowers. Now he sees authority rather differently—"a dog's obeyed in office."

38. Gloucester, cured of suicidal thoughts, thinks Edgar is a kind beggar. Oswald, delivering a letter, tries to capture Gloucester, but Edgar kills him and reads the letter. Goneril and Edmund plan to kill her husband.

39. Cordelia, who has had Lear under doctor's care, now tries to restore him gently to sanity. Kent, who is now known for who he really is, prepares to meet Edmund, who is commanding the enemy army.

40. Regan proposes to Edmund (who has already proposed to Goneril). Edgar brings Goneril's husband, Albany, the letter he took from Oswald about the plot to murder him.

41. Edmund has won the battle, and Lear and Cordelia are prisoners. They don't seem afraid of prison—they have each other—but they should be. Edmund sends a man after them.

42. Albany wonders who the "guard" is, then turns on Edmund, who is a subject, not yet a brother-in-law. Regan defends him, but Albany orders his arrest. Edmund challenges Albany, who calls . . .

Shakespeare Made Easy

King Lear

43. . . . a masked champion—Edgar. Regan feels sick as the men begin to fight. Edmund loses, and when Goneril tries to interfere, Albany shows her the letter. Goneril leaves in a hurry.

44. As Edgar unmasks and tells how he survived and tended Gloucester, a servant rushes in to say that Goneril poisoned Regan and committed suicide. Edmund, dying, laughs that he can now "marry" both.

45. Kent comes in looking for Lear and Cordelia. Edmund gasps out that he has sent orders to kill them in their cells. Edgar rushes out to stop the killing, but he's too late.

46. Lear staggers in with the body of Cordelia in his arms. He kneels, not believing that she is dead, trying to see if her breath will cloud a mirror.

47. Kent tries to get Lear to recognize him, and tells him that Goneril and Regan are dead, but Lear scarcely listens. Albany offers to resign while Lear lives, but . . .

48. . . . Lear, still hoping against hope that Cordelia is alive, dies. Albany offers the realm to Kent and Edgar, but Kent is too brokenhearted to want anything. It is left to Edgar to form the new order.

Shakespeare Made Easy

King Lear: Quick Quiz

1. What is the contest that King Lear proposes for his daughters? _____
   _____

2. How is Cordelia not altogether a loser in Lear's contest? _____
   _____

3. How does Edmund plan to get rid of his brother? _____
   _____

4. What is Goneril's objection to Lear's behavior? _____
   _____

5. How do Goneril and Regan band together against Lear? _____
   _____

6. Why is Gloucester so upset at what Lear's daughters have done? _____
   _____

7. How does Gloucester disobey orders? _____
   _____

8. What is the unexpected result of Gloucester's punishment? _____
   _____

9. Why does Albany defend Goneril and fight in a war he doesn't like? _____
   _____

10. What does Edmund realize about marrying either Goneril or Regan? _____
    _____

11. Why does Edgar let Gloucester "jump" from the "cliff"? _____
    _____

12. What dishonorable order does Edmund give after the battle? _____
    _____

13. How does Edgar get his revenge? _____
    _____

14. Why does Kent not want to revive Lear? _____
    _____

15. How does Edgar end up being the ruler? _____
    _____

Macbeth

Macbeth

Introduction

Have you ever wanted something very badly, then discovered once you got it that it wasn't what you wanted after all?

Have you ever told a lie which trapped you into a whole series of lies and cover-ups?

Have you ever let a friend do something wrong because you might profit from it?

The temptations that Macbeth succumbs to are not peculiar to medieval Scotland. We've all wanted something, envied someone, bent the truth, or watched a friend do something foolish.

Macbeth

1. The play begins with three witches talking about meeting Macbeth. Why Macbeth? Do they know something we don't know?

2. Macbeth, we hear, is the hero of Scotland. He has saved the aging King Duncan's realm by winning two battles in one day and killing the rebel leader by himself. Why would the witches be interested in him?

3. As Macbeth and his second in command, Banquo, go back to base, they meet the witches, who greet Macbeth as Thane of Glamis, Thane of Cawdor, and "king hereafter." Banquo, they say, will be "lesser than Macbeth, and greater," "not so happy, yet much happier"; his sons will be kings, though he will not. Having amazed the generals, the witches vanish. Poof!

4. Macbeth's imagination begins to run wild. He is Thane of Glamis by birth and he has just defeated the Thane of Cawdor's troops in battle. Kings could be elected and he's the most likely candidate—if Duncan were to die. Banquo tries to warn Macbeth that witches are witches and don't go around doing good, but Macbeth doesn't listen.

5. Just then messengers arrive from the king, announcing that Macbeth has been given the title of Thane of Cawdor. That's two out of three: Macbeth becomes a believer in the witches' words.

6. Duncan showers honors on Macbeth and decides that, since his realm is now free from enemies, he can name his young son Malcolm as his heir. Now Macbeth cannot hope to succeed to the throne when the old man dies.

Macbeth

7. Macbeth sends his wife a letter to tell her of the witches' prophecies and his new title. She knows him well enough to know he will need a push to do what he wants—kill the king and take his place.

8. Having decided that they will kill the king that very night, the Macbeths prepare for his arrival. Lady Macbeth is *so* nice to the old man as she greets and ushers him into the castle.

9. During dinner Macbeth has second thoughts and leaves the table—a breach of etiquette. Lady Macbeth follows, confronts him, and changes his mind.

10. As he waits for his wife's signal that the "coast is clear," Macbeth reassures the apprehensive Banquo. Then Macbeth sees a ghostly dagger covered in blood. Does this deter him? No.

11. Macbeth stabs Duncan to death while Lady Macbeth waits outside. He is so upset by his deed that he doesn't notice that he has carried the knives belonging to the drugged guards—the murder weapons—away.

12. Lady Macbeth returns the daggers to Duncan's room (she intends to accuse the guards), getting her hands all covered in blood, too. When she returns, she hears knocking at the gate. She and Macbeth go off to change into nightclothes to pretend they've been asleep.

Shakespeare Made Easy

13. The porter takes a long time to open the gate because he's drunk. (The servants have been celebrating, too.) He pretends he's answering the doors of hell.

14. The people appointed to awake the king, Macduff and Lennox, discover his body. The castle is in an uproar as everyone crowds in to see the horror.

15. When the questions (such as why did Macbeth kill the guards) become too sharp, Lady Macbeth faints. Whether the faint is real or faked, it distracts Banquo and Macduff. The crowd breaks up, getting no answers to the murder.

16. Malcolm and Donalbain, the king's two sons, realize that anyone who murdered the king will not stop there. They flee the country, Malcolm going to England and Donalbain to Ireland.

17. When we next see the Macbeths, they are king and queen. Macbeth questions Banquo about where he is going and when, because Macbeth intends to kill him and his son, Fleance. Banquo knows too much. Remember the prophecies?

18. Three murderers ambush Banquo on his way home and kill him, but Fleance escapes. The murderers report to Macbeth, who indicates that he doesn't intend to stop with this one killing. But he won't tell Lady Macbeth, who's next on his hit list.

Shakespeare Made Easy

Macbeth

19. At the evening's banquet, Macbeth plays "I know something you don't know" with the lords, who are very nervous of him. He proposes a toast, wishing Banquo were at the feast.

20. To Macbeth's horror, the ghost of Banquo takes him up on his invitation. No one else can see Banquo's ghost, so Macbeth's reaction is inexplicable to the guests. Then Lady Macbeth takes charge and sends the guests home.

21. Knowing now that he is so evil he can call up a ghost, Macbeth seeks the help of the witches. He finds them brewing a spell by throwing various nauseating ingredients into a pot.

22. The first apparition they conjure up for Macbeth is a head in a helmet that warns, "Beware Macduff!" (Guess who Macbeth has next on his hit list.)

23. The second apparition is a baby covered in blood. It says, ". . . [no man] of woman born shall harm Macbeth." Although he now thinks he's invincible, does Macbeth take Macduff off his hit list? No.

24. The third apparition is a crowned child carrying a branch. It tells him he will never be defeated until Birnam Wood comes to Dunsinane Castle. Then Macbeth asks one question too many . . . .

Shakespeare Made Easy

25. "Will Banquo's children ever reign?" he asks. As an answer, the ghost of Banquo shows him a long line of kings. Enraged, Macbeth orders the murder of Macduff, but he has already escaped to England. He orders everyone Macduff left behind killed: wife, children, servants, the Scottie dog—everyone.

26. Although warned, Lady Macduff cannot flee with an entire household in time. She waits for the murderers, who kill her young son in front of her. She (and he) are the first entirely innocent persons to die; now the people know no one is safe in Macbeth's Scotland.

27. Malcolm has grown up into a rather formidable young man and Macduff is trying to get him to come back to Scotland. When Macduff hears the news of the slaughter, he cannot believe it. Then he and Malcolm decide to make it their rallying cry. England lends them an army.

28. Meanwhile, Lady Macbeth has gone mad. She sleepwalks around the castle, rubbing at the "blood" she fantasizes is still staining her hands. She talks of the other murders, too, so that what she says is so dangerous no one will dare to help her.

29. As Malcolm's army approaches, people desert Macbeth's army, leaving him with too few troops for a battle. He rants and raves on the battlements of Dunsinane Castle. He still has absolute faith in the apparitions' prophecies.

30. Malcolm, now in command of a large army, orders his soldiers to cut down tree branches in Birnam Wood to conceal their numbers.

Macbeth

31. A messenger reports Lady Macbeth's suicide. Another tells Macbeth of the moving grove. Suddenly Macbeth realizes the true nature of the prophecies. Instead of lying doggo in the castle, he decides to fight.

32. Macduff searches the battlefield for Macbeth and will not fight anyone else.

33. Finally Macduff and Macbeth meet. In a last spark of decency, Macbeth warns his enemy of the prophecy, only to find that Macduff was delivered by Caesarean operation, not "born." Macduff offers to let Macbeth surrender, but, even though he knows it's hopeless, Macbeth chooses to fight.

34. The play ends with Macduff presenting Macbeth's head to Malcolm and being the first to call him the King of Scotland. Malcolm swears to rule justly and well.

Macbeth: Quick Quiz

1. From what two perils has Macbeth just saved Scotland? _____
   _____

2. What are the witches' three prophecies for Macbeth? _____
   _____

3. What are the witches' three prophecies for Banquo? _____
   _____

4. What is Lady Macbeth's plan to make the prophecies come true faster? _____
   _____

5. How do we know Banquo suspects the Macbeths of the murder? _____
   _____

6. Why does Fleance's escape ruin Macbeth's plan? _____
   _____

7. Who can see Banquo's ghost at the banquet? _____
   _____

8. What are the apparitions' set of three prophecies? _____
   _____

9. Why is Malcolm so suspicious of Macduff? _____

10. What did Macduff never suspect would happen? _____
    _____

11. What has happened to Lady Macbeth? _____
    _____

12. How do the apparitions' prophecies come true? _____
    _____

Measure for Measure

Measure for Measure

Introduction

Can a judge be above the law?

Is a crime still a crime if it is done for a good purpose?

How much can you ask a person to sacrifice for love?

Measure for Measure is a play in which no one is uncorrupted and leaders resort to underhanded subterfuges or abuse their power. It's an uncompromising look at how power, sex, and even religion can corrupt—a play for today's world.

Measure for Measure

1. The play begins with Vincentio, the Duke of Vienna, bidding farewell. He's off to a monastic retreat, leaving his deputies, Angelo and Escalus, to clean up the city in his absence.

2. Angelo's rule soon falls hard on lawbreakers. Mistress Overdone, a brothel keeper, tells of a young gentleman, Claudio, being arrested for fornication—then she learns all the brothels are to be torn down.

3. Lucio meets his friend Claudio as Claudio is being taken to prison. From him we get a different story of the "fornication." He and Juliet were not married because of a legal complication with her dowry.

4. Claudio realizes that Angelo, as the new authority figure, will probably make an example of him. He sends Lucio to get his sister—who is about to enter a nunnery—to plead his case.

5. But the Duke hasn't gone away! He has dressed himself up like a friar so he can watch Angelo enforce the laws that he (the Duke) has ignored for nineteen years.

6. Isabella is about to enter the convent joyfully when Lucio arrives and tells her of her brother's danger. Isabella agrees to go back "into the world" to beg Angelo's mercy for her brother.

7. Even though Escalus, the Duke's other deputy, pleads for Claudio, Angelo says he has broken the law and is to be executed tomorrow morning.

8. Constable Elbow, who has trouble with words, brings in Froth and Pompey, two of the brothel staff. Pompey's defense is so long that Angelo leaves Escalus to deal with it.

9. Froth and Pompey are luckier than Claudio. Escalus lets them off with a warning, although it is clear that they have broken Vienna's anti-fornication laws. Pompey doesn't intend to heed his warning.

10. The Provost has come to see Angelo to find out if Claudio really is to be executed tomorrow morning. Angelo tells him it's none of the Provost's responsibility, then admits Isabella.

11. Isabella loves her brother, but finds it hard to plead for him because she cannot condone what he has done. She accepts Angelo's dictum that Claudio must die, but Lucio doesn't. He tells her to ask again.

12. Isabella pleads for mercy, reminding Angelo that when he is judged he would like God to be merciful. The law condemns Claudio to die tomorrow, Angelo says. Isabella is horrified.

13. Isabella asks Angelo if he has never done any-thing wrong, then offers to bribe him—with maid-en's prayers. Angelo takes a second look at her and tells her to come back later.

14. Alone, Angelo realizes that he's awfully attracted to Isabella because of her virtue. Will he recall his own sentence on her brother to please her? He doesn't know.

15. The Duke, now disguised as a friar, visits Juliet in prison. She admits she still loves Claudio and that their sin was mutual. She too is devastated that Claudio is to die tomorrow.

16. Angelo cannot stop thinking about Isabella. When she comes to see him again, he proposes that he could put off the date of Claudio's death indefin-itely—if Isabella will sleep with him.

17. Horrified, Isabella, the almost-nun, refuses. How does Angelo dare propose the crime her brother is condemned for? Isabella threatens to tell, but Angelo asks, who would believe her? Isabella goes to tell Claudio of her refusal.

18. The Duke/friar is comforting Claudio when Isabella arrives, so he eavesdrops on their conversation. Isabella asks Claudio if he is prepared to die to-morrow. Then she tells him of Angelo's proposal—and her refusal.

19. At first Claudio thinks Isabella is right, but when he thinks that the reality of death tomorrow could be traded for her honor, he pleads with her to take Angelo's offer. Isabella is aghast.

20. The Duke/friar interrupts and tells them that this was a test Angelo devised for Isabella's virtue. Claudio apologizes to her. Alone with Isabella, the Duke/friar proposes a solution.

21. Angelo cruelly jilted Mariana. The Duke/friar proposes that Isabella agree to meet Angelo in a dark place of her choosing, and have Mariana, who still loves Angelo, take her place. Isabella agrees.

22. The Duke/friar meets Constable Elbow, who has rearrested Pompey. As the Duke/friar berates Pompey, Lucio happens along and falls into conversation with the "friar."

23. Lucio comments on how cold Angelo is and says that the Duke was not like that—the Duke liked women and wine. Lucio says he was a personal friend of this "superficial" fellow and knows why he left.

24. No sooner has Lucio left than Escalus enters, taking Mistress Overdone to prison. The "friar" asks Escalus's opinion of the Duke. Escalus calls him temperate and selfless, but is too worried by Claudio's fate to say much more. The Duke vows to "get" Angelo.

25. Mariana, Isabella, and the "friar" plan how the bed trick is to be accomplished. Mariana agrees to help Isabella save Claudio, because she considers Angelo her husband by their pre-contract.

26. Pompey agrees to become the executioner's assistant, but Abhorson, the executioner, thinks a bawd will disgrace executing as a profession. As the night draws on, the Provost and the friar await Claudio's pardon.

27. Angelo's message comes: execute Claudio five hours early, and the other prisoner, Barnardine, later in the afternoon. To buy some time, the Duke/friar convinces the Provost to execute Barnardine instead and present his head as Claudio's.

28. Barnardine, who is rather drunk, refuses to be executed. Happily, another prisoner who looks quite like Claudio has died of fever. His head is sent to Angelo. But the Duke/friar doesn't tell Isabella.

29. Instead, the Duke/friar lets Isabella believe Claudio is dead. He tells her that the Duke knows all about this and is coming home tomorrow. He gives Isabella letters to deliver.

30. Angelo and Escalus receive the letters, which tell them to meet the Duke outside the gates—where anyone who feels they have been unjustly treated may petition them. Escalus isn't worried—but Angelo is.

Shakespeare Made Easy

31. The Duke, now in his ducal robes, greets Angelo. Their exchange of pleasantries is interrupted by Isabella, who accuses Angelo of murder, virgin-violation, etc. Angelo says she's a madwoman.

32. Isabella tells her story (aided by Lucio). The Duke asks who put her up to this, then arrests her. Lucio doesn't make the situation any better by casting aspersions on Friar Lodowick (the Duke).

33. Then Mariana accuses Angelo and tells of the switch of ladies. Angelo denies this and asks if he can punish the woman to find out what's behind these "false accusations." The Duke agrees and leaves.

34. When the Duke returns, dressed as Friar Lodow-ick, he is accused of inciting Mariana and Isabella to slander Angelo. Lucio tries to ingratiate himself by accusing the friar of saying awful things about the Duke. He pulls off the friar's hood . . . to find the Duke.

35. Shocked, Angelo confesses to the Duke, who sends him to marry Mariana immediately. He forgives Isabella, and, when Angelo returns, condemns him to death. Mariana pleads, and Isabella pleads for her—after all, her brother had justice.

36. The Provost brings in two prisoners, one covered. The Duke pardons Barnardine, gives Claudio back to Isabella, and asks (demands?) her hand in marriage. He commends Escalus and the Provost, then condemns Lucio to marrying a prostitute, whipping, and hanging—a problematical ending.

Shakespeare Made Easy

Measure for Measure: Quick Quiz

1. Why is the Duke leaving Angelo and Escalus in charge of Vienna? _____
   _____

2. How does the Duke lie to Angelo and Escalus? _____
   _____

3. How does Isabella get involved? _____
   _____

4. What trade does Angelo offer Isabella? _____
   _____

5. How does the Duke find out about Angelo's offer? _____
   _____

6. Why does Mariana agree to the "bed trick"? _____
   _____

7. What is the similarity between the Duke and Pompey? _____
   _____

8. How does Angelo keep his part of the bargain? _____
   _____

9. What accident saves Barnardine? _____
   _____

10. Why does the Duke let Isabella think Claudio is dead? _____
    _____

11. What is Angelo's defense when Mariana and Isabella accuse him? _____
    _____

12. What happens to Angelo? _____
    _____

13. What happens to Isabella? _____
    _____

14. What happens to Lucio? _____
    _____

A Midsummer Night's Dream

A Midsummer Night's Dream

Introduction

What do you do when your parents are going to force you to marry the boy *they* like—not the boy *you* like?

What do you do when you fall in love with your girlfriend's best friend, but she hasn't got the time of day for you?

How do you get anything accomplished when you have a loudmouth know-it-all in the group?

A Midsummer Night's Dream is a lighthearted comedy about love and marriage—all kinds of love and marriage. Love that's returned and love that's spurned. Marriages of state, marriages of love, and marriages on the rocks—to say nothing of marriages that may never happen if Hermia's father has his way.

A Midsummer Night's Dream

1. The town of Athens is decorated to celebrate the marriage of Duke Theseus to Hippolyta, Queen of the Amazons. Egeus, a courtier, threatens to ruin the celebrations by demanding his legal right— that his daughter (Hermia) marry the man of his choice, or be buried alive.

2. Theseus reluctantly invokes the law, but gives Hermia time to think over her decision to die rather than marry Demetrius. She uses the time to tell the man she loves, Lysander, that she loves him still. The lovers decide to flee Athens, but they're overheard by Helena, who is in love with Hermia's spurned suitor, Demetrius. Confused? Just wait. . . .

3. Helena thinks that the news of the lovers running away will make Demetrius fall out of love with Hermia (and in love with her). But it doesn't. He follows them into the woods.

4. So Helena decides to follow Demetrius, who is following Hermia and Lysander. Meanwhile . . .

5. At the home of Peter Quince, a group of mechanicals (working people) meets to rehearse a play for the wedding. Bottom thinks he can play all the parts, but settles for the lead. To keep the play a surprise, the group decides to rehearse in the woods . . . .

A Midsummer Night's Dream

6. Meanwhile, in the woods, nature is upset by an argument going on between Oberon and Titania, king and queen of the fairies, over a changeling child they both claim.

7. After Titania refuses to give up the child, Oberon sends his attendant spirit, Puck, to find a love potion. Then he overhears Demetrius threaten Helena to make her stop following him. Oberon decides to do something about this.

8. Oberon enchants Titania by squeezing love juice into her eyes as she sleeps so she will fall in love with the first thing she sees when she wakes up. (Oberon hopes it is something ugly.)

9. Puck, sent to enchant Demetrius into loving Helena, stumbles upon Lysander and Hermia. He assumes these are the two Athenians Oberon described and puts love juice on Lysander's eyes.

10. Helena, who has lost Demetrius, finds Lysander and wakes him up. Guess what? Immediately Lysander is madly in love with Helena. Unnerved, Helena flees.

11. Lysander looks at his former love Hermia and can't stand her. He leaves her in the middle of nowhere to follow Helena. Hermia wakes up, finds herself alone, and goes to find Lysander. Meanwhile . . .

12. The mechanicals arrive to rehearse in the woods. Bottom still thinks he can play all the parts (which would be just fine with Flute, who doesn't want to play Thisbe, the girl). Eventually Bottom goes into the bushes to await his entrance as the romantic lover Pyramus.

13. There mischievous Puck puts an ass's head on top of Bottom. When he enters on his cue . . .

14. . . . the mechanicals flee in terror from the "translated" Bottom. The noise wakes up Titania, who falls in love with the first thing she sees—guess who?

15. Oberon is delighted with Puck's joke. He's not so delighted when he sees what's happening with the Athenian lovers.

16. Demetrius catches up with Hermia, only to have her accuse him of doing away with her beloved Lysander. Puck realizes he's put the juice on the wrong Athenian.

17. Demetrius, worn out by exercise and rejection, lies down and falls asleep. Oberon enchants him with the love juice.

Shakespeare Made Easy

18. Demetrius is woken up by Helena, who is still trying to get rid of the lovesick Lysander. Guess what?

19. Helena thinks the two enchanted young men are playing a practical joke on her. Hermia arrives and interprets the situation very differently.

20. Enjoying her newfound popularity, Helena picks a fight with Hermia, who is only too glad to oblige. Helena runs away, chased by Hermia. Demetrius and Lysander chase after the two girls. Puck finds their behavior hilarious.

21. Puck leads the four through the woods so they don't hurt themselves or each other, then charms them all to sleep near each other. He removes the love charm from Lysander's eyes.

22. Now that Titania has given up her changeling child, Oberon thinks his joke has gone on long enough. He removes the love charm from her eyes and they are reconciled.

23. Comes the dawn . . . . The four young lovers are awakened by the royal lovers, Theseus and Hippolyta, who are out hunting. It is the royal wedding day and they are so happy they overrule Egeus and decree that the young lovers will be married at the royal ceremony, too.

24. Left alone, the young lovers try to remember what happened the previous night—but they can't.

25. Bottom, who has also been "decharmed," wakes up and decides he has had a fabulous dream.

26. Back at Peter Quince's house, the mechanicals welcome Bottom—once they make sure he's alive. Now they can put on their play for the Duke.

27. Philostrate, the emcee for the wedding reception, tries to convince Theseus not to see the mechanicals' awful play. Theseus looks beyond the ham-handed dramatics to the "simpleness and duty" that caused the men to offer this as a wedding present.

Shakespeare Made Easy

28. The mechanicals' play, "Pyramus and Thisbe," is really dreadful. It's a tragedy about two young lovers who are separated by a wall. Pyramus sees Thisbe's bloodstained scarf where they are to meet and assumes she's been eaten by a lion. He kills himself with great fanfare, then Thisbe discovers his body and kills herself. (It's very dramatic stuff but hardly a choice for a wedding.)

29. Keeping a straight face, Theseus thanks the players. He asks for a dance rather than any more of their play, then, when the dance is over, leads the newlyweds to bed.

30. Oberon and Titania fly through the darkened palace, scattering fairy grace and good luck on the three couples and the children they will have.

31. The audience gradually returns to our real world as Puck speaks the epilogue and explains that this was all . . . a midsummer night's dream.

Shakespeare Made Easy

A Midsummer Night's Dream: Quick Quiz

1. Why does Egeus want to bury his daughter alive? _____
   _____

2. Why does Helena tell Demetrius that Hermia and Lysander are running away? __
   _____

3. Why is the weather in the forest unnatural? _____
   _____

4. Why do the mechanicals go to the forest? _____
   _____

5. What trick does Oberon play on Titania? _____
   _____

6. How does Lysander fall in love with Helena? _____
   _____

7. Why is Oberon delighted with Puck's trip? _____
   _____

8. How does Hermia escape her fate? _____
   _____

9. Why is the mechanicals' play chosen? _____
   _____

10. What is wrong with the play? _____
    _____

11. How does the Duke excuse the amateur nature of the mechanical's play? _____
    _____

12. How do the fairies bring the play to an appropriate end? _____
    _____

Othello

Othello

Introduction

Have you ever been wrongly accused of something and been unable to defend yourself because people were too upset to listen?

Have you ever lost a present that meant much more to the giver than it did to you?

Have you ever had someone suggest something about a friend that completely changed your view of that friend—so much that you could no longer maintain the friendship?

Othello isn't a play about racism as much as it is a play about jealousy, conflicting values, and the power of suggestion.

Othello

1. Iago and Roderigo both have grudges against Othello (Iago because another man, Cassio, has been given the post he wants; Roderigo because he's jealous of Othello's success with Desdemona). They revenge themselves by waking Brabantio and telling him his daughter Desdemona has run away to Othello.

2. In the very next scene, Iago is apparently Othello's friend as Othello confronts the enraged Brabantio. Another group which is searching for Othello arrives and all go to the Senate.

3. The Duke has sent for Othello because the Turkish fleet is about to attack the Venetian stronghold of Cyprus. The Duke realizes he will have to deal with Brabantio's enraged accusations first.

4. Desdemona is summoned to tell her side of the story, and when she arrives it's clear she is in love with Othello. Brabantio, despite his earlier hospitality to the victorious general, is horrified that his daughter has actually married a black man. He withdraws angrily.

5. The Senate sends Othello out to deal with the Turkish threat. Meanwhile, Roderigo is desolate but Iago sidles up and says the marriage won't last. He advises Roderigo to make money for the day Desdemona will tire of her Moor.

6. Alone, Iago ponders what to do. He hates Othello because he thinks Othello has been his wife Emilia's lover. He hates Cassio for his promotion. If only he can persuade Othello that Desdemona and Cassio are lovers . . . .

7. In Cyprus, Montano, the governor, waits for the Venetian fleet. First to arrive is Cassio, then Desdemona, Emilia, and Iago. To make the time pass (and disguise their nervousness about Othello's delay) the group discusses women. Iago is not impressed, but Cassio is gallant.

8. At last Othello arrives with the good news that the storm that delayed his ship sank the Turkish fleet. Othello and his news receive a grateful welcome.

9. Iago is still working on Roderigo. Tonight Cassio and Iago are on watch. Iago directs Roderigo to watch Cassio and, if he sees a chance, pick a quarrel with him. Roderigo isn't sure . . . .

10. Later that night, Iago manages to get Cassio to take one drink too many. After Cassio staggers out, Iago remarks to Montano, the ex-governor, that it's a pity Cassio is often like this.

11. Suddenly Cassio comes back, chasing Roderigo. Montano tries to intervene, saying that Cassio is drunk. Cassio takes offense and fights him. Montano is wounded.

12. Othello arrives and stops the fight. He is furious with Cassio. Iago, while claiming he doesn't want to tell tales, tells what happened in a way that shows Cassio in a very bad light. Othello relieves Cassio of his command. The only way to get back his post and honor, Iago advises, is to get Desdemona to plead his case.

13. First thing next morning, Cassio is trying to get his job back. He speaks to Desdemona (in Emilia's presence) and she promises to plead his case to Othello. Iago is delighted.

14. No sooner does Othello arrive than Desdemona starts to ask him to reinstate Cassio. She is so persistent that Othello tells her to give him a minute to himself. In that minute Iago is there, insinuating that Cassio and Desdemona used to know each other *very* well.

15. Warning Othello to beware of jealousy, Iago conjures up the "green-eyed monster," saying that an outlander like Othello can't understand a subtle Venetian like Desdemona. After all, she deceived her father to marry Othello. Othello wavers and asks Iago to get Emilia to spy.

16. Iago points out that Desdemona's championing of Cassio was a little too enthusiastic. When Desdemona brings an invitation to Othello, he is so upset that he bats her hand away and her pretty handkerchief falls, unnoticed, as Desdemona worries over him.

17. Emilia finds the handkerchief and remembers that it was Othello's first gift and that Iago wants her to steal it. She is reluctant to turn it over to her husband, knowing how upset Desdemona will be when she misses it, but she does give it to Iago.

18. Othello (silly man) confides his confusion, jealousy, and anger to Iago, who is very sorry to hear it. Then Iago mentions that Cassio talks in his sleep—about Desdemona—and uses a strawberry-patterned handkerchief rather like Desdemona's.

     Shakespeare Made Easy

Othello

19. That's it! Othello flies into a rage against Cassio and Desdemona. Iago pledges to help, saying that in three days Cassio will be dead—but don't kill Desdemona, he says, thus planting the idea in Othello's mind.

20. Desdemona is really upset that she's lost the handkerchief, but doesn't think Othello will mind. Wrong! Othello crashes in and demands the "magic" handkerchief. Desdemona is too frightened to confess she's lost it, so she lies about its whereabouts. He stomps out.

21. Iago brings in Cassio, who has come to see how Desdemona's pleading is getting along. Desdemona says Othello's not himself today—it must be worries of state. Emilia says he might be jealous, but Desdemona refuses to consider the idea—there's no cause.

22. Cassio meets Bianca, a "lady of the evening" who is in love with him, and asks her to copy the needlework on the pretty handkerchief he found in his room. Bianca wonders where he got it, but Cassio is too concerned with getting back into Othello's favor to bother with such trivia.

23. Iago is still working on Othello, so successfully that the general falls into an epileptic fit. (Iago is enjoying this!) When Othello recovers, Iago hides him where he can see and later overhear Iago's talk with Cassio.

24. Iago gets Cassio to talk about Bianca, but Othello thinks he's talking about Desdemona. Just then Bianca herself enters and throws the handkerchief at Cassio, accusing him of having another lover. Cassio follows her to keep her quiet.

Shakespeare Made Easy

25. Othello has seen the handkerchief—he wants Desdemona dead. When Iago suggests that Othello strangle her in the bed she has "contaminated," he thinks that's a fitting idea.

26. Just then Lodovico, a Venetian with a letter for Othello, comes in, accompanied by Desdemona. While Othello reads the letter, Lodovico inquires after the absent Cassio and learns of his demotion.

27. Desdemona mentions that she would like Othello and Cassio to be friends again "for the love I bear to Cassio." (Talk about unfortunate word choice!) Othello hits her. Everybody gasps.

28. Othello, so furious he can barely speak, humiliates Desdemona in front of the disbelieving Lodovico. When both have gone, Iago confides that Othello has been behaving strangely—if not madly.

29. Othello quizzes Emilia about Desdemona's relationship with Cassio and Emilia denies it utterly. But by this time Othello is so jealous he shrugs Emilia's testimony off as a lie.

30. Othello then confronts Desdemona, who denies any wrongdoing. Finally, he calls her a whore and throws some coins at her. Emilia tries to comfort Desdemona, and suspects that someone is behind the accusation and Othello's actions.

31. Meanwhile, Roderigo has given up on his quest for Desdemona. He wants Iago to get the jewelry that he's given her (through Iago) back. Iago says there's one last chance. If he kills Cassio . . . .

32. Othello now seems calmer, but Desdemona isn't fooled. She orders the wedding sheets put on the bed, and sings a song associated with love and death in her family.

33. Iago and Roderigo await Cassio. Roderigo attacks Cassio and both he and Cassio are wounded. Othello says that Iago is keeping his word, and leaves to murder Desdemona. Only now does Roderigo realize how he's been used by Iago.

34. Iago has raised the alarm and, with Lodovico and Gratiano, discovers both combatants wounded, not dead. Iago kills Roderigo before he can say anything. Bianca rushes to the wounded Cassio while Iago comments on how guilty she looks.

35. Othello looks down at the sleeping Desdemona. Now he sees her death more as justice than vengeance. Desdemona awakes and realizes what Othello intends. In vain she pleads for more time. Othello smothers her.

36. Emilia comes in to tell of the attack on Cassio but she stops, horrified, when she sees Desdemona's body. Othello repeats his accusations. Emilia refuses to believe, but when Othello tells her that Iago told him all this, she begins to understand.

Shakespeare Made Easy

37. Iago, Gratiano, and the rest arrive. Emilia turns on Iago, accusing him of responsibility for Desdemona's death. She tells what really happened with the handkerchief. To shut her up, Iago stabs her.

38. Everyone is so stunned that Iago escapes. Othello puts the dying Emilia on the bed beside Desdemona. The rest take his sword and lock him in while they pursue Iago.

39. But Othello has another sword, so that when the pursuers bring in Iago, Othello attacks and wounds him before he is disarmed again. Othello confesses that he was fooled by Iago.

40. Besides Emilia's and Othello's accusations, there's more evidence against Iago. Letters have been found on Roderigo's body: one is from Iago, directing Roderigo to kill Cassio; the other is Roderigo's complaint about the setup that got Cassio demoted.

41. Lodovico removes Othello from command, making Cassio ruler of Cyprus, and demands that Othello return to Venice for justice. Iago is to be tortured into confessing.

42. Othello isn't quite defeated. He pulls out a dagger and, proclaiming himself one who loved not wisely but too well, kills himself. His body falls onto the bed, across Desdemona and Emilia. Cassio says he suspected Othello would do something like this because he was "great of heart." The play ends.

Name: _____ Date: _____

Othello: Quick Quiz

1. Why does Iago hate both Cassio and Othello? _____
   _____

2. Why is Roderigo helping Iago? _____
   _____

3. Why does the Duke support Othello in his disagreement with Desdemona's
   father? _____
   _____

4. How does Cassio fall into disgrace? _____
   _____

5. What is unwise about Desdemona's pleading for Cassio? _____
   _____

6. What does Othello accept as proof of Desdemona's infidelity? _____
   _____

7. How does Roderigo become a liability to Iago? _____
   _____

8. What goes wrong with the kill-Cassio plan? _____
   _____

9. How do we know that Desdemona suspects that Othello will kill her? ____
   _____

10. How does Emilia choose between Iago and Desdemona? _____
    _____

11. How does Roderigo have the last laugh on Iago? _____
    _____

12. How does Othello salvage some honor out of the mess his jealousy has created?
    _____
    _____

Shakespeare Made Easy

Romeo & Juliet

Romeo and Juliet

Introduction

What would happen if you fell in love with someone you knew your parents and friends would not approve?

What would you do if the two people you trusted and counted on most failed you in a crisis?

What would you do if for the rest of your life you had to face the consequences of something stupid you'd done in anger?

No wonder *Romeo and Juliet* is staged so often. Girls still fall in love with the "wrong" boys; boys still fall in love with the "wrong" girls. Adults still fail the young; the young are still naive and impulsive. People haven't changed much since Shakespeare's time, as a reading of *Romeo and Juliet* will attest.

Romeo & Juliet

1. The play begins as a peaceful morning is disrupted by a brawl between the servants of the Montagues and the servants of the Capulets. This is not the first time it's happened, either.

2. The Prince of Verona arrives, breaks up the brawl, and summons the heads of the feuding families. He warns that the next brawl will be paid for with their heads.

3. Romeo Montague, our hero, isn't in the brawl. He's been out for an early morning walk, sighing over Rosaline, his lady love. (He's never spoken to her.)

4. Meanwhile, Juliet Capulet is being told of her father's plans for her marriage to Paris, the prince's cousin. (Quite a catch!)

5. Romeo, cousin Mercutio, and some friends crash the party the Capulets are giving (where Romeo hopes to see his beloved Rosaline). Tybalt, the Capulets' hot-tempered nephew, spots them—but Capulet refuses to let him start a fight about it. (Guess why.)

6. Sometime during the dance, Romeo sees Juliet and Juliet sees Romeo—love at first sight! They don't know—until it's too late—that he is the only son and she is the only daughter of the feuding families.

Shakespeare Made Easy

7. After the party, Juliet thinks she's alone and speaks of her newfound love for Romeo. He is in the garden and overhears her. They end up pledging undying love and planning marriage.

8. Romeo rushes off to tell his friend/mentor Friar Laurence. The friar, at first skeptical, thinks he sees a way of ending the feud: if he can present the only son married to the only daughter, the feud will *have* to be called off.

9. Juliet is given a message through her nurse, comes to the church, and Friar Laurence marries the young couple. Nobody but these four knows of the wedding.

10. Meanwhile, Tybalt, still angry about last night's party-crashing, picks a fight with Romeo's cousin Mercutio.

11. Romeo, who is too happy to fight with anybody, tries to separate Tybalt and Mercutio. Tybalt's sword goes under Romeo's arm to fatally wound Mercutio. Mercutio dies with a curse and a pun.

12. Too angry to think straight, Romeo pursues, duels with, and kills Tybalt—Juliet's cousin.

13. The Prince, furious that his law has been broken, also realizes that both families have lost loved ones. He contents himself with banishing Romeo.

14. Juliet is distraught when she hears that her brand-new husband has killed her cousin. (There is no chance of reconciling the families now.) She carries on and on . . . .

15. The newlyweds spend one night together, then Romeo leaves to begin his banishment.

16. The Capulets are upset by Juliet's moping around and wrongly attribute it to her mourning Tybalt. They decide to cheer her up by marrying her to Paris—the day after tomorrow.

17. Juliet refuses to marry Paris. After a terrible fight with her parents, they tell her to marry Paris or get out (whichever suits her). Remember, nice girls couldn't marry without a dowry, and besides, Juliet is already married. To marry Paris would be the crime (if not the sin) of bigamy. Friar Laurence offers one hope—a catatonic potion.

18. Juliet takes the potion and is discovered "dead" on the morning of her wedding. The celebration changes to mourning as Juliet is buried in the family vault. The plan is that Friar Laurence will be there to let her out when she wakes up, and will spirit her out of the city to join Romeo . . . . But . . .

Romeo and Juliet

19. . . . Romeo's servant sees Juliet's funeral and rides to tell his master. Friar Laurence's messenger is delayed, so the servant reaches Romeo first.

20. Convinced that life without Juliet is meaningless, Romeo buys poison from a down-and-out apothecary. Then he goes to join Juliet.

21. At the Capulet family tomb, he meets Paris, who is also mourning Juliet. They fight, and the hapless Paris is killed. Then Romeo breaks into the vault.

22. There, by Juliet's bier, he makes a short tragic speech, takes his poison, and dies.

23. Friar Laurence arrives too late. When Juliet wakes up, she sees Romeo's body. They hear the watchmen coming, but Juliet refuses to leave. (Friar Laurence runs away.) Juliet joins her Romeo by committing suicide with his dagger.

24. The next morning, the Montague-Capulet feud ends as the families bury their only children.

Shakespeare Made Easy

Name: _____   Date: _____

Romeo and Juliet: Quick Quiz

1. What is the Prince's ruling about brawls in Verona? _____
   _____

2. What happens to Romeo's feelings for Rosaline at the Capulets' party? _____
   _____

3. When do Romeo and Juliet realize that they come from rival houses? _____
   _____

4. Why does Friar Laurence agree to marry Romeo and Juliet? _____
   _____

5. How does Mercutio die, and what does this prompt Romeo to do? _____
   _____

6. How does Juliet's father try to cheer her up? _____
   _____

7. What dilemma does the impending marriage pose for Friar Laurence? _____
   _____

8. Why does Friar Laurence's messenger not reach Romeo in time? _____
   _____

9. Why does Paris try to arrest Romeo? _____
   _____

10. How does Friar Laurence fail Juliet? _____
    _____

11. What do Prince Escalus and company find in the tomb? _____
    _____

12. What symbolizes the end of the Montague-Capulet feud? _____
    _____

The Taming
of the Shrew

The Taming of the Shrew

Introduction

Have you ever felt that your parents loved a brother or sister better than you?

Have you ever seen through the social games people play and refused to play them?

Have you ever tried to attract attention by being outrageous?

If you have, you've experienced the problems that Kate, the Shrew, faces in the play *The Taming of the Shrew*. No matter what she does, Kate's father sides with her younger sister, Bianca. Kate won't play all the games Bianca plays—she demands that people accept her for who she is, not what they want her to be. Does she sound familiar? Will she be tamed? Read on and find out.

Shakespeare Made Easy

The Taming of the Shrew

1. The story begins when the lord, who has been out hunting, discovers Sly fast asleep. He decides to play a trick on him.

2. When Sly wakes up, everybody bows to him as a lord, until he begins to believe it. A play is to take place in his honor.

3. The play begins with Lucentio arriving in Padua with his servants, Biondello and Tranio. He's there to study, but forgets all about that when he sees the fair Bianca, who is being courted by Hortensio and old Gremio. But Baptista, Bianca's father, won't hear of her marriage until Kate, her older sister, finds a husband—and that won't be easy.

4. Lucentio, who has heard Baptista ask for tutors for Bianca, decides to be one, leaving his servant Tranio to take his place.

5. Meanwhile, Hortensio's outrageous friend Petruchio arrives in town and says he's looking for a rich wife. Hortensio says he knows just the woman.

The Taming of the Shrew

6. Before the scene is over, Hortensio has decided to dress up as a music tutor, Gremio has hired Lucentio as a Latin tutor for Bianca (and incidentally to talk up Gremio), and Tranio has presented himself as Lucentio. All go to court Bianca.

7. Kate is amusing herself by tormenting Bianca. She's realized that whatever she does her father will prefer Bianca—what's the point in even *trying* to be sweet and nice?

8. When the suitors arrive and Petruchio explains he is there to woo Kate, Baptista is delighted. They make a deal about dowry then and there. But Baptista wants Kate to consent.

9. Kate, meanwhile, has smashed the new lute over Hortensio's head. This doesn't deter Petruchio, so everyone clears out, leaving the arena to him and Kate.

10. Their first meeting does not bode well for a tranquil relationship. The more rude and angry Kate is, the more complimentary Petruchio is. Even when her father returns, Petruchio is complimentary and says he wants to marry her still.

11. Baptista is so delighted he's at last found a husband for Kate, he sets the wedding for next Sunday—despite Kate's protests. Petruchio says he must go to Venice to prepare, and Bianca's suitors rejoice. She will marry one of them the following Sunday.

Shakespeare Made Easy

12. Bianca is enjoying the attention of her two young and handsome "schoolmasters." Lucentio tells her who he is and why he's there. How romantic!

13. Sunday arrives. Kate waits at the altar, and waits . . . and waits . . . .

14. Finally Petruchio arrives—not looking at all the way a bridegroom should. Nevertheless, they are wed.

15. Petruchio wins the first battle of the marriage by carrying Kate away from her own wedding reception—before she's even been to it.

16. Grumio, Petruchio's servant, tells his fellows what a terrible journey they've had from Padua. Everything has gone wrong, and now they've arrived home and nothing is ready for them.

17. Kate and Petruchio, famished and dirty from their awful journey, sit down to dinner, but Petruchio "kills Kate with kindness." He finds fault with every dish served, so Kate gets nothing to eat.

   Shakespeare Made Easy

18. Hortensio sees that Bianca isn't interested in him. Tranio convinces him to give up and court a rich widow, leaving the field open to his master Lucentio.

19. Then Tranio, who must produce a father if he is to get Baptista's permission to marry Bianca (for Lucentio), convinces a pedant to play the part.

20. Meanwhile, at Petruchio's, Kate still hasn't had anything to eat. All her rages and demands have been ignored by the servants.

21. Kate finally gets dinner, then Petruchio sees the dress he's ordered for Bianca's wedding. It's not fine enough, he says, and tears it to shreds. They'll go in what they have on. (Kate is getting her just deserts: she's on the receiving end of her typical behavior.)

22. Tranio presents his "father" to Baptista (who's a lot more careful about Bianca's bridegroom than Kate's!). Baptista gives "Lucentio" his consent.

23. On the way to Bianca's wedding, Kate and Petruchio meet Vincentio, Lucentio's real father, and have some fun with him. He too is on his way to Padua.

Shakespeare Made Easy

24. Vincentio goes to Lucentio's house, to be met by "Vincentio." He begins to be really worried when he meets "Lucentio."

25. Just as Tranio convinces everyone that Vincentio is a lunatic (and Vincentio is convinced Tranio has murdered his son) Lucentio and Bianca turn up—married.

26. Kate and Petruchio, Bianca and Lucentio, and Hortensio and a rich widow celebrate the wedding feast. But during the celebrations the others begin to tease Petruchio for having been stuck with a "shrew." He makes a bet: Send for your wives and the winner is the man whose wife comes. Lucentio and Hortensio send; Bianca and the widow refuse.

27. It is Kate who comes, forcibly leading the other two. Now that she's found her soul-mate, it's Kate and Petruchio against the world. The play ends.

28. Sly falls asleep. The lords and players leave. When he wakes up he wonders if it all was a dream.

       Shakespeare Made Easy

Name: _____ Date: _____

The Taming of the Shrew: Quick Quiz

1. Why won't Baptista let Bianca get married? _____

   _____

2. How does Lucentio decide to get closer to his lady love? _____

   _____

3. Why is Petruchio interested in Katharina, not Bianca? _____

   _____

4. How does Hortensio decide to get closer to his lady love? _____

   _____

5. How are Kate's wooing and wedding similar? _____

   _____

6. How does Petruchio "kill Kate with kindness"? _____

   _____

7. Why does Tranio hire the pendant? _____

   _____

8. What does Lucentio's father think when he gets to Padua? _____

   _____

9. Who get married and celebrate the wedding feast? _____

   _____

10. How does Petruchio win his bet? _____

    _____

    _____

The Tempest

The Tempest

Introduction

Have you ever found it more difficult to forgive someone who injured someone you love than to forgive someone who injured you?

Have you ever met someone so concerned with his or her status or possessions that he or she works it into the first few minutes of every conversation?

Have you ever fantasized about the perfect revenge?

We've all thought about what we should have done or said as the perfect comeback to an injury or insult. Prospero, the main character in *The Tempest*, has had thirteen years to brood over what he should have done and how he should get back at the people who injured him and his beloved daughter, Miranda. But when he finally gets a chance at revenge, he finds all his painstaking plans come out quite differently.

The Tempest

1. The play begins with a ship sinking in a fearful storm. While the mariners work frantically to save the ship, some of the passengers curse at them, others stay out of their way and pray, and one makes feeble jokes.

2. On the island, Miranda is distressed by seeing the shipwreck. She goes to her father, Prospero, a sorcerer, and asks him why he's raised the storm. He assures her that everybody on the ship is safe.

3. Prospero decides it's time to tell Miranda how they got to the island they've been marooned on for 13 years. He once was the Duke of Milan, but, loving to study, he neglected his administration, giving most of the work to his brother, Antonio.

4. Soon Antonio decided he wanted the title that went with the job, so he staged a coup with the help of the neighboring king, Alonso. Prospero was deposed and cast adrift to drown—and Miranda was, too.

5. The only person who behaved kindly to them was Gonzalo, who provisioned the boat and gave Prospero his favorite books to take with him. All of these men are on the ship in the storm.

6. Prospero charms Miranda asleep and calls his attendant spirit, Ariel. Ariel reports that she (?) terrified the sailors and deposited the king's party around the island. Ariel is reluctant to do more; Prospero first threatens her, then promises her freedom.

Shakespeare Made Easy

The Tempest

7. Prospero wakes up Miranda and they visit Caliban, a savage man-beast now kept in check since he tried to rape Miranda. Caliban resents Prospero, because Caliban owned the island before Prospero arrived.

8. Caliban is sent away to work, and Ariel leads in Ferdinand, the king's son, with a song. Ferdinand thinks he is the only survivor of the shipwreck. Then he sees Miranda . . . .

9. Miranda, whose acquaintance with men is limited to Caliban and her father, falls in love with Ferdinand immediately, as he does with her. So their love will not be untested, Prospero pretends to be angry with Ferdinand and enslaves him.

10. On another part of the island, King Alonso and his courtiers are looking for Ferdinand but are losing hope. Antonio and the king's brother, Sebastian, amuse themselves with nasty remarks aimed at Gonzalo, who is at least trying to be positive about their predicament.

11. Ariel enchants the courtiers to sleep, all but Antonio and Sebastian. "Now's your chance," argues Antonio, convincing Sebastian to murder his brother to become king. (Does who is king matter on a desert island?) They plan to kill Gonzalo, too.

12. Just as they draw their swords, Ariel wakes up the king, Gonzalo, and the others. Antonio and Sebastian, caught with their weapons drawn, say they heard scary noises. The group continues its search.

Shakespeare Made Easy

13. Caliban, out collecting wood, sees Trinculo the jester and mistakes him for one of Prospero's spirits. Trinculo, seeking shelter from an approaching storm, thinks Caliban has been killed by lightning and crawls under his cape.

14. Stephano, the king's butler, reels up to the caped figures. (He's found a butt of sherry [144 imperial gallons] and refuses to drink water until he's finished the sherry.) First he thinks he too has caught an islander—a live one with four legs and two voices.

15. When Caliban and Trinculo get untangled, Stephano offers them sherry. Caliban has never tasted such stuff and vows Stephano shall be his god. (Trinculo is not sure he likes this.)

16. Ferdinand is doing menial labor—piling logs. Miranda offers to do it for him, then proposes to him. Seeing he is dealing with no ordinary girl, Ferdinand pledges his love to her. Prospero, looking on, approves.

17. Stephano, Trinculo, and Caliban have gotten drunker (if it's possible). Ariel, invisible, picks a fight between Trinculo and Caliban, which forms a comic parody of the verbal fighting that goes on in the court party.

18. Then Caliban changes the tone of things. He tells the others about Prospero and Miranda and begs Stephano to murder his former master. Stephano agrees so he'll be "King of the isle."

19. Meanwhile, the court party is still searching for Ferdinand, but old Gonzalo can go no farther. Alonso orders the party to rest; as they do so, islanders in strange shapes present them with a banquet.

20. But just as they are to eat the food, it vanishes, and Ariel appears as a harpy. Only the three who have harmed Prospero can see it, but Gonzalo guesses that their strange actions (drawing their swords in pursuit of nothing) are a result of their "great guilt."

21. Back at Prospero's cave, the sorcerer explains that he has only been testing Ferdinand and Miranda's love, and now he approves. He gives them a vision of goddesses as a wedding present.

22. The vision is interrupted by Ariel's warning that the drunks are approaching, with murder on their minds. Prospero stops the masque-vision and explains it was all an illusion—rather like a play. Miranda and Ferdinand leave him alone.

23. Ariel reports that she has led the drunks around the island, finally dumping them into the cesspool. Then Prospero has her hang out a line of fancy garments as bait.

24. The stinking drunks arrive and see the beautiful clothes. Stephano and Trinculo bicker over who gets what, while Caliban says this is all trash—get on with killing Prospero! But it's too late. Prospero sics his spirits (in the shapes of hounds) on them.

25. Now Prospero has everyone exactly where he wants them. He's given each group a vision and a test and everyone (including Ferdinand) is at his mercy.

26. But Prospero sees that Ariel is upset. Old Gonzalo, she reports, is crying for the distress of Alonso. She would pity the people Prospero torments—if she were human.

27. Suddenly Prospero realizes that if he repays harm with harm he is no better than Antonio, Alonso, and the others who have hurt him. He has come *so* close to abusing his great powers that he decides he cannot handle them and must give them up.

28. But first he must clear up the problems on the island. He has Ariel bring in the court party, who stand before him, unseeing and enchanted, until the magic ebbs away.

29. Prospero sends Ariel for his ducal robes so that when Alonso comes to his senses, he is confronted by the man he has wronged. Immediately, Alonso begs Prospero's forgiveness.

30. Not everyone is capable of remorse. Antonio and Sebastian do not ask forgiveness. Prospero doesn't punish them, but takes back his dukedom from his brother.

The Tempest

31. Alonso says he has lost his son in the storm; Prospero says he has lost his daughter. Alonso wishes they were alive and that they were King and Queen of Naples. Then Prospero grants his wish by drawing back the curtain to the cave and showing him both children, alive.

32. Now we find out what Prospero meant when he said he lost his daughter, for now she has a husband. When Miranda comes out she sees only beauty in mankind (including Antonio and Sebastian). Prospero doesn't correct her—she must learn on her own now.

33. Alonso gladly accepts Ferdinand's decision to marry Miranda, and Gonzalo rejoices at how strangely things have come right. The ship's boatswain comes in to tell that the ship is enchanted, safe, and seaworthy.

34. Stephano and Trinculo reel in, reeking and hung over. Caliban has never seen Prospero in his robes before and the contrast between Prospero and Stephano convinces him he was wrong to worship Stephano.

35. Prospero acknowledges Caliban and sets him to work off his penance, which Caliban does willingly this time because he understands why he must work. Prospero prepares to go back to Milan and frees Ariel.

36. Now, Prospero says, he has no power but his own, having given up his magic. He asks the audience to forgive him, free him, and fill the sails of the ship to send it home—by clapping.

The Tempest: Quick Quiz

1. Why has Prospero created the tempest? _____

   _____

2. Who are Ariel and Caliban? How do they differ? _____

   _____

3. What is Miranda's reaction to Ferdinand? What does Prospero do about it? ____

   _____

4. Why do Antonio and Sebastian attempt to murder Alonso and Gonzalo? _____

   _____

5. How does Caliban react to Stephano? What does he want Stephano to do? _____

   _____

6. Why can't Gonzalo see the harpy which appears to Antonio, Sebastian, and
   Alonso? _____

   _____

7. Who interrupts the wedding masque? How are they dealt with? _____

   _____

8. Why doesn't Prospero carry out his plan? _____

   _____

9. How does Prospero show his forgiveness of Alonso? _____

   _____

10. How does Prospero lose Miranda? _____

    _____

11. How does Caliban feel about Prospero when he sees him in his proper robes? ___

    _____

12. What is Prospero asking the audience for in the epilogue? _____

    _____

Twelfth Night

Twelfth Night

Introduction

What do you do when the boss asks you for a date—you don't want to go out with him, but you don't want to lose your job, either.

How do you handle someone who thinks he's better than you are because he believes he's more moral?

What would you do if you were marooned in a strange land, with no chance of getting home for months, or even years?

These problems don't sound much like the stuff of comedy, but they're only some of the problems of *Twelfth Night*'s characters, and they're still valid today. We might experience sexual harassment, or have to endure holier- (or smarter- or fitter- or more athletic) -than-thou moralists. We wonder what might happen if we were stranded in a strange city—without even having a charge card. How would we cope? Follow the misadventures of Olivia, Sir Toby Belch, and Viola, and see . . . .

Twelfth Night

1. The play begins with Orsino, Duke of Illyria, who is lovesick for the Lady Olivia. She greets his overtures of love by telling his messenger she will be in mourning for her brother for seven years. Does this discourage Orsino? No. Not a bit.

2. Meanwhile, the Lady Viola has been rescued from a shipwreck and thinks she's the only survivor: her brother's missing. She cannot compromise her reputation by going to Orsino's bachelor court, and Olivia's mourning has closed her house, so . . .

3. . . . Viola dresses as a page boy and gets a job at Orsino's court. Soon he is so delighted with his new page that Orsino sends "Cesario" to woo Olivia for him. There's one complication: Viola wouldn't mind being wooed by the Duke, herself.

4. But the Duke is not the only one wooing Olivia. Sir Andrew Aguecheek is being groomed by Olivia's ne'er-do-well uncle, Sir Toby Belch, to marry Olivia (and her money). Meanwhile, Sir Andrew is paying Sir Toby's considerable bar bills.

5. Also in Olivia's house are Malvolio, the manager or steward, and the person who irritates him most, Feste the jester.

6. Only Feste can point out to Olivia that her mourning for her brother's soul is really mourning for her own loss of him—if she believes her brother's soul is in heaven. Feste sees things more clearly than most characters, and as the fool he can say what others cannot.

Shakespeare Made Easy

7. Olivia, bored with her self-imposed confinement, decides to have some fun with Orsino's latest unwanted messenger of love. She covers her face with her veil and sits with her servants. Though it is obvious from their dress which is the lady of the house, "Cesario" (Viola) won't play Olivia's little game.

8. They fence with words, and finally Olivia throws back the veil, expecting admiration. Cesario admits she's pretty "if God did all," i.e., if her beauty is not from cosmetics. This is NOT how Orsino's messengers are supposed to react. Olivia takes a second look at this unusual page.

9. Olivia tells Cesario that she cannot love Orsino, then asks "him" what "he" would do if "he" were in love. Well, Cesario/Viola *is* in love, and her account of what she would do for love makes Orsino's love poetry sound as phony as a $3 bill. Olivia takes a third look at this unusual "young man."

10. After asking a few questions about "his" background, Olivia sends Cesario back to Orsino. She suddenly realizes how attracted to him she is. She calls Malvolio and gives him a ring to give to Cesario. At least "he" will have to come back to return it.

11. Malvolio, angry at being used as a messenger boy, delivers the ring rather rudely. Cesario realizes what the ring means—that Olivia fancies "him." This will complicate Viola's life, but she can't afford to abandon her Cesario disguise yet.

12. Meanwhile, back at the seacoast, Viola's twin brother, Sebastian, has arrived after being rescued by another sea captain, Antonio. Sebastian mourns his drowned sister, and decides to try his fortune in Illyria. Antonio, though he is a wanted man there, decides to follow Sebastian.

Shakespeare Made Easy

13. Late, late that night Sir Andrew and Sir Toby roll into Olivia's house. They ask Feste for a song and are soon joined by Maria, who has come down to tell them to be quiet. Their songs get louder, until . . . .

14. . . . Malvolio appears. He says Olivia is most annoyed and would be happy if Toby would leave the house. When Toby ignores him, Malvolio turns on Maria and scolds and threatens her.

15. Angry at Malvolio's throwing his weight around, the party people plot revenge. Maria proposes that she write a letter which will imply the writer is in love with Malvolio—and her writing is just like Olivia's.

16. Next morning, the Duke is still swanning around. He sends for Feste (because lovers love to hear love songs). Feste's song says the ultimate gesture of love is to die for it—but the Duke doesn't get the message.

17. Cesario (Viola) tries to explain to Orsino that he can't *make* Olivia love him, but Orsino refuses to admit he can't. So Cesario tries another tactic, talking about a mythical "sister" who loved a man so much she died of it, meaning women can feel love as strongly as men. The Duke ignores this, too.

18. Meanwhile, Malvolio is in the garden practicing his courtly behavior. While Sir Andrew, Sir Toby, and Fabian (a servant Malvolio has ratted on) eavesdrop, Malvolio fantasizes what it would be like to be married to Olivia.

Shakespeare Made Easy

YELLOW STOCKINGS

19. Malvolio finds the letter Maria has planted and, sure enough, he doesn't even consider that it could be a practical joke. He's convinced that Olivia loves him, and vows to show her he's interested by doing what the letter asks—smiling, wearing yellow stockings, and all.

20. Cesario comes to Olivia's house to court her for Orsino yet again. On the way there "he" encounters Sir Andrew and Sir Toby. Although "he" gets as good as he gives in a duel of words with Feste, "he" easily defeats the Sirs in a duel of wits.

ULP!

A DUEL   HOME

21. Unfortunately for Cesario, Olivia is no longer shy. She proposes to "him" but Cesario can only promise that "his" heart has been given to no woman.

22. Sir Andrew sees Olivia react to the page as she's never reacted to him, and decides to go home. Sir Toby and Fabian convince him to challenge Cesario to a duel instead.

LOOK!

HI, SWEETIE

23. Meanwhile, Antonio and Sebastian have come to town. Sebastian wants to sightsee, but Antonio, who has a price on his head, is nervous. He lends Sebastian all his money and heads for an inn so he won't be seen.

24. Meanwhile, Malvolio appears before Olivia, smiling and wearing yellow stockings. He takes whatever she says as encouragement.

Shakespeare Made Easy

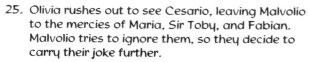

25. Olivia rushes out to see Cesario, leaving Malvolio to the mercies of Maria, Sir Toby, and Fabian. Malvolio tries to ignore them, so they decide to carry their joke further.

26. Sir Andrew brings his challenge in for Sir Toby's approval, which provides more fun. Sir Toby promises to deliver the letter to Cesario, but . . .

27. . . . Sir Toby convinces Cesario that Sir Andrew is a fatally good duelist, then convinces Sir Andrew that Cesario has been fencing instructor to the Shah of Persia. Both "combatants" are terrified of each other—to Sir Toby's great amusement.

28. But Sir Toby's joke is ruined by the entrance of Antonio, who intervenes to save the person he thinks is Sebastian.

29. The fight attracts two officers who arrest Antonio. Needing money for prison, Antonio asks for his money back, addressing Cesario as Sebastian. Viola/Cesario doesn't have his money, but she realizes what the request must mean—that Sebastian is alive.

ANACHRONISM

30. Meanwhile, convinced that Cesario is a coward, Sir Andrew vows to fight "him" again and beat "him" to win Olivia's love.

EEK!

EN GARDE!

31. Unfortunately, Sir Andrew picks a second fight with Sebastian, who, because he has been educated as a gentleman (unlike Viola), knows how to fight.

32. This duel too is interrupted. Olivia stops the fight and starts to speak to Sebastian as though she knows him very well. Sebastian doesn't mind this at all.

33. While this is going on, Feste, Maria, and Toby amuse themselves by tormenting Malvolio, who has been imprisoned in a dark place (the standard treatment for lunatics). First Feste comes in as a priest . . .

HOWL!

34. . . . Then Feste goes to the cellar as himself. Malvolio wants to write to Olivia *so* badly that he is even nice to his enemy, the fool.

35. The next time Olivia meets "Cesario," she's prepared. She proposes marriage. A slightly bemused Sebastian accepts, and Olivia produces a priest (a real one) who will marry them . . . now.

36. The Duke reconsiders his strategy of courting Olivia by messenger and comes to her. He meets Feste, who is carrying a letter, and bids him to fetch Olivia. He expects Olivia to be overwhelmed.

37. As he waits, Orsino questions Antonio, who sounds quite sane until he insists that Cesario has been his constant companion for the last three months.

38. Contrary to his expectations, Olivia is distinctly underwhelmed by the Duke's presence. She has eyes only for Cesario.

39. The Duke puts two and two together and comes up with a two-timing Cesario. All Viola/Cesario's protests are in vain—especially when Olivia calls "him" husband.

40. Suddenly the tense situation is interrupted by Sir Andrew, who clutches a bloody handkerchief to his head. He claims he and Sir Toby have *just* been beaten up—by Cesario.

41. As Sir Toby and Sir Andrew limp off, Sebastian runs in, chasing them. His entrance causes a sensation which he assumes is because of his drawn sword. He's glad to find Antonio.

42. Suddenly Sebastian sees Cesario. It takes him a while to realize that the page is the sister he had given up as dead.

43. Olivia discovers she's married Sebastian instead of Cesario, but doesn't seem too upset.

44. The Duke, realizing Cesario is actually a woman, suddenly knows what all her talk of love was about. He proposes to Viola. Suddenly Viola wants her woman's apparel, but the sea captain who has it has been imprisoned by Malvolio.

45. "Prison" and "Malvolio" remind Feste of the letter, which Fabian reads aloud. The letter doesn't sound as though it was written by a madman. Olivia sends for Malvolio, who arrives brandishing "Olivia's" letter.

46. Malvolio thrusts the letter at Olivia, who examines it and says it's in Maria's writing, not hers. Fabian and Feste explain the practical joke played on Malvolio and announce that Sir Toby is so pleased he's married Maria. Publicly humiliated, Malvolio vows revenge "on the whole pack" of them.

47. Malvolio stomps off. The lovers go off in pairs. The officers free Antonio, and Feste ends the play with a song.

Name: _____ Date: _____

Twelfth Night: **Quick Quiz**

1. Why does Olivia tell the Duke's messenger she'll be in mourning for seven years?
   _____

2. What dilemma is Viola facing when she lands in Illyria? _____
   _____

3. How does Viola's solution to her dilemma become a problem when she visits Olivia for the Duke? _____
   _____

4. Why do Sir Toby, Sir Andrew, Maria, and Feste play the letter trick on Malvolio?
   _____

5. What does the "love letter" tell Malvolio to do? _____
   _____

6. Why does Malvolio fall for the love letter? _____
   _____

7. Why does Sir Toby have Sir Andrew challenge Cesario? _____
   _____

8. Why is Antonio arrested? _____
   _____

9. Why is Sebastian surprised to meet Olivia? _____
   _____

10. How does Feste torment Malvolio when he is locked in the cellar? _____
    _____

11. What does the Duke propose to do to Olivia and Cesario when he thinks he discovers they're married? _____
    _____

12. How does Sebastian's sudden entrance clarify things? _____
    _____

13. How does the Duke realize that he's been foolish? _____
    _____

14. How is Malvolio's humiliation better than the conspirators could hope? _____
    _____

15. Who is the third married couple? _____
    _____

The Winter's Tale

The Winter's Tale

Introduction

What do you do when your king (or boss, or commanding officer) orders you to do something that he'll regret later?

How do you deal with the accusations of someone who is beyond the reach of reason?

How do you live with yourself when your stupidity has hurt the people you love?

The Winter's Tale is a play about making bad judgments and dreadful mistakes, then having a chance to atone and put things right—almost. King Leontes is responsible for the death of his wife, his son, and his infant daughter, and the exile and death of his most trusted counselors. He is given a second chance—a chance to "put Humpty Dumpty back together again"—almost. We've all done things we regret, and we dream of having a second chance.

The Winter's Tale

1. King Polixenes of Bohemia has come to spend an extended vacation with his childhood friend, King Leontes of Sicilia, and Leontes' wife, Queen Hermione.

2. Soon Polixenes and Hermione get along so well that suspicions begin to dog Leontes.

3. Leontes tells his trusted counselor Camillo that he suspects Polixenes is the father of Hermione's child. He wants Polixenes dead.

4. Camillo, knowing Polixenes and Hermione are innocent, tells Polixenes of Leontes' murderous plan. Both flee to Polixenes' kingdom.

5. There is no such escape for Hermione, who is thrown into prison.

6. Leontes has a difficult time explaining to his son Mamillius what he's done.

7. Sure of his accusations, Leontes sends envoys to the oracle at Delphi for a condemnation to use at Hermione's trial.

8. When Hermione's child is born, the king will have nothing to do with it. He orders it taken to Polixenes' country and abandoned on the seacoast.

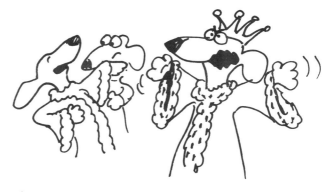

9. But the news from the oracle is not what he expects. The oracle says Hermione is innocent.

10. Leontes refuses to believe the oracle! Hermione faints and is carried from the shocked court.

11. Then the news comes, news that confirms the oracle's dire predictions—that Leontes is a tyrant and kills his nearest and dearest. Hermione has died and their little son Mamillius has died of grief.

12. Leontes realizes how wrong he's been.

Shakespeare Made Easy

13. But it's too late.

14. On the seacoast of Bohemia, Antigonus reluctantly abandons the infant, whom he has named Perdita (the lost one). On his own initiative he adds some gold, and a scroll that tells who she is.

15. The seacoast is a wild place; faithful Antigonus is pursued (and eaten) by a bear.

16. A poor shepherd discovers Perdita and decides to adopt her even before he sees the gold, which will make him a comparatively wealthy man. He also finds the scroll, but he can't read.

17. Sixteen years pass . . . .

18. In Sicilia, Leontes has never remarried. He spends his time with Paulina, Antigonus's widow, remembering those dear ones they've lost (and whose fault that was!).

Shakespeare Made Easy

19. Meanwhile, in Bohemia, Polixenes is becoming curious about where his son, Prince Florizel, goes. He and Camillo put on disguises and follow him.

20. As Polixenes feared, Florizel has become involved with a girl: he has become engaged to a charming shepherdess (guess who) who doesn't know he's the prince.

21. It's shearing festival time, and Autolycus, a rogue, arrives to fleece the simple shepherds.

22. Perdita treats the two strangers at her shearing feast with great courtesy, but Polixenes still finds her an unsuitable match for Florizel. He reveals his identity and forbids Florizel to marry his "low-born" darling.

23. Camillo convinces Florizel and Perdita to elope to Sicilia. (He really wants to go back because he's homesick.)

24. To disguise the prince, Camillo has Florizel trade garments with Autolycus.

Shakespeare Made Easy

25. The Old Shepherd and his son, afraid of the king's anger, get out the "fardel," the robe and scroll Perdita was found with, to explain she's not really a relative. They enlist "courtier" Autolycus to help them.

26. Soon Polixenes, furious, follows Camillo, Perdita, and Florizel to Bohemia. He's followed by the two shepherds and Autolycus, who want to explain that Perdita's a foundling.

27. Leontes welcomes Florizel and Perdita with open arms. Having wronged the father, Leontes tries to repay the son. (He's sure that Perdita reminds him of someone, too.)

28. When Polixenes arrives in a rage, Leontes (who knows what terrible things can be done in anger) calms the irate father. Eventually Polixenes consents to the marriage.

29. The shepherds arrive with the scroll which tells us who Perdita really is. The lost one is found!

30. Now, the reunited families go to see a statue of Hermione that Paulina has had set up in her house. The statue is very realistic.

31. When faithful Paulina draws back the curtain, not a statue but Hermione ALIVE is revealed. Leontes is overjoyed and Hermione meets her daughter.

32. The young lovers are united as prince and princess . . . with Polixenes' blessing.

33. Leontes is given a second chance with Hermione . . . .

34. Paulina (now that she knows what has happened to Antigonus) marries Camillo . . . .

35. The shepherds are justly rewarded . . . .

36. And everyone is happy . . . . Even Autolycus.

Shakespeare Made Easy

The Winter's Tale: Quick Quiz

1. For how long have Leontes and Polixenes been such good friends? _____
   _____

2. What triggers Leontes' jealousy? _____
   _____

3. What dilemma does Leontes' order pose for Camillo?_____
   _____

4. What does Leontes order done with his infant daughter? _____
   _____

5. What does Leontes expect the oracle's message to contain? _____
   _____

6. How does the oracle's prophecy come true immediately? _____
   _____

7. Why is it important that the Old Shepherd adopt the baby before he sees the bag
   of gold?_____
   _____

8. Why is Polixenes angry at Florizel? _____
   _____

9. How is Polixenes' order about Perdita as unfair as Leontes'?_____
   _____

10. Why does Camillo help Florizel and Perdita escape? _____
    _____

11. What does the Old Shepherd's fardel contain? _____
    _____

12. How could Hermione's ''statue'' come alive?_____
    _____